Contents

Summary

1. The results of social innovation - new ideas that meet unmet needs - are all around us. They include fair trade and restorative justice, hospices and kindergartens. Many social innovations were successfully promoted by the Young Foundation in its previous incarnations under Michael Young (including some 60 organisations such as the Open University, Healthline and International Alert).

2. Over the last two centuries, innumerable social innovations, from neighbourhood policing to Wikipedia, have moved from the margins to the mainstream (and on page 15 we provide our list of ten world-changing social innovations). As this has happened, many have passed through the three stages that Schopenhauer identified for 'every truth': 'First, it is ridiculed. Second, it is violently opposed. Third, it is accepted as being self-evident.' These processes of change are sometimes understood as resulting from the work of heroic individuals (such as Robert Owen or Muhammad Yunus); sometimes they are understood as resulting from much broader movements of change (such as feminism and environmentalism). Here we look at how innovations have progressed through a series of stages: from the generation of ideas through prototyping and piloting, to scaling up and learning. We look at how in some sectors key stages are missing or under supported. We also show that in some cases innovation starts by doing things – and then adapting and adjusting in the light of experience. Users have always played a decisive role in social innovation – a role which is increasingly recognised in business too. In all cases, innovation usually involves some struggle against vested interests; the 'contagious courage' that persuades others to change; and the pragmatic persistence that takes promising ideas into real institutions.

3. Social innovation is not unique to the non-profit sector. It can be driven by politics and government (for example, new models of public health), markets (for example, open source software or organic food), movements (for example, fair trade), and academia (for example, pedagogical models of childcare), as well as by social enterprises (microcredit and magazines for the homeless). Many of the most successful innovators have learned to operate across the boundaries between these sectors and innovation thrives best when there are effective alliances between small organisations and entrepreneurs (the 'bees' who are mobile, fast, and cross-pollinate) and big organisations (the 'trees' with roots, resilience and size) which can grow ideas to scale.

4. Economists reckon that 60-80% of economic growth comes from innovation and new knowledge.[1] Although there are no reliable metrics, innovation appears to play an equally decisive role in social progress. Moreover, social innovation plays a decisive role in economic growth. Past advances in healthcare and the spread of new technologies like the car, electricity or the internet, depended as much on social innovation as they did on innovation in technology or business. Today there are signs that social innovation is becoming even more important for economic growth. This is partly because some of the barriers to lasting growth

THE YOUNG Y FOUNDATION

Social Silicon Valleys

a manifesto for social innovation:
what it is, why it matters and how it can be accelerated

Spring 2006

Acknowledgements

This report has been published with support from the British Council in Beijing. As well as having been prepared to help guide the work and action of the Young Foundation, which was relaunched in 2005, it is also part of the lead up to a major international conference on social innovation to be held in Beijing in late 2006 jointly with the British Council and the China Centre for Comparative Political Economy. (The conference website, which will combine case studies, comments and discussion is www.discoversocialinnovation.org.) We are grateful to the various supporters of the Young Foundation's practical work in this field, in particular Morgan Stanley and the Baring Foundation who have supported Launchpad, as well as Cisco, the Corporation of London, Philips Design, SAP, BP and Vertex and the Joseph Rowntree Charitable Trust. We are grateful for comments from many sources and in particular for helpful steers from Marcial Boo, Eric Rasmussen, Tony Flower, Hilary Cottam, Michael Frye, Charles Handy, Rosabeth Moss Kanter, Gary Hallsworth, Eric Von Hippel, John Kao, Graham Leicester, Robin Murray, Ed Mayo, Martin Sime, Nick Temple, John Thackara and Karl Wilding; and discussions with a range of groups including the Danish Government, the Scottish Parliament, the International Futures Forum, the Australia and New Zealand School of Government, Said Business School, and the World Economic Forum. Useful discussions were also held in various cities across the UK, as well as in Seoul, Singapore, Stockholm, Beijing and Chongxing.

Authors

This paper has been written by Geoff Mulgan with Young Foundation colleagues Nick Wilkie, Simon Tucker, Rushanara Ali, Francis Davis and Tom Liptrot. We would very much welcome comments for a revised version which will be published later this year.

The Young Foundation
17-18 Victoria Park Square
Bethnal Green
London E2 9PF
+44 (0) 20 8980 6263
youngfoundation.org

Printed by The Basingstoke Press
ISBN 1-905551-01-0 / 978-1-905551-01-9
First published in 2006 ©The Young Foundation

(such as climate change, or ageing populations) can only be solved with social innovation, and partly because of rising demands for growth that enhances human relationships and well-being.

5. Surprisingly little is known about social innovation compared to the vast amount of research into innovation in business and science. Some of the insights gained into business innovation are relevant in the social field, but there are also important differences. We argue that the lack of knowledge impedes the many institutions interested in this field, from individual philanthropists and foundations to governments, and means that far too many rely on anecdotes and hunches. Lack of reliable knowledge about common success factors and inhibitors also makes it harder for innovators themselves to be effective and for ideas to be improved into a sustainable form.

6. Although social innovation happens all around us, we argue here that far too many promising ideas are stillborn, blocked by vested interests or otherwise marginalised. The competitive pressures that drive innovation in commercial markets are blunted or absent in the social fiend and the absence of institutions and funds devoted to social innovation means that too often it is a matter of luck whether ideas come to fruition, or displace less effective alternatives. As a result, many social problems remain more acute than they need to be, with all that implies for human suffering: these include (but are far from being limited to) the problems associated with ageing and climate change, and the rising incidence of chronic disease, conflict and poverty.

7. In this manifesto we advocate a much more concerted approach to social innovation, and have coined the phrase 'Social Silicon Valleys' to describe the future places and institutions that will mobilise resources and energies to tackle social problems in ways that are comparable to the investments in technology made in the first silicon valley and its equivalents around the world. This is likely to require major changes amongst governments, foundations, Non Governmental Organisations and business, including :

- New sources of finance focused specifically on innovation, including public and philanthropic investment in high risk R&D, targeted at the areas of greatest need and greatest potential.

- More open markets for social solutions, including public funding and services directed more to outcomes and opened up to social enterprises and user groups as well as private business.

- New kinds of incubator for promising models, along the lines of the Young Foundation's Launchpad programme, and what we call 'accelerators' to advance innovation in particular areas such as, for example, chronic disease or the cultivation of non-cognitive skills.

- New ways of empowering users to drive innovation themselves – with tools, incentives, recognition and access to funding for ideas that work.

- New institutions to help orchestrate more systemic change in fields like climate change or welfare – linking small scale social enterprises and projects to big institutions, laws and regulations (for example, shifting a city's transport system over to plug-ins or hybrids).

- New approaches to innovation for individual nations, cities and regions that cut across public, private and non-profit boundaries, including cross-national pools to develop and test new approaches to issues like prison reform or childcare.

- New institutions focused on adapting new technologies for their social potential – such as artificial intelligence, grid computing or Global Positioning Systems.

- New ways of cultivating the innovators themselves – drawing on experiences from organisations like the School for Social Entrepreneurs.

8. To inform practical initiatives we argue for more extensive, rigorous, imaginative and historically aware research on how social innovation happens and how it can be helped.

9. This manifesto is deliberately preliminary. It describes a work in progress and is designed to bring together others interested in taking this work forward. It also provides the context for the Young Foundation's emerging role as a small, but hopefully effective, catalyst for social innovation – linking research and action, and designing, launching and, in time, scaling up new enterprises and new models. Finally, it provides some inputs for a growing international network of like-minded organisations sharing ideas and experiences with the aim of speeding up our collective ability to treat, and even solve, some of the pressing social challenges of our times.

Social innovation: an introduction

The growing importance of social innovation

The results of social innovation are all around us. Self-help health groups and self-build housing; telephone help lines and telethon fundraising; neighbourhood nurseries and neighbourhood wardens; Wikipedia and the Open University; complementary medicine, holistic health and hospices; microcredit and consumer cooperatives; charity shops and the fair trade movement; zero carbon housing schemes and community wind farms; restorative justice and community courts. All are examples of *social* innovation - new ideas that work to meet pressing unmet needs and improve peoples' lives.

This manifesto is about how we can improve societies' capacities to solve their problems. It is about old and new methods for mobilising the ubiquitous intelligence that exists within any society.

Over the last two decades there has been a great deal of progress in the understanding and practice of social enterprise and entrepreneurship, which has prompted the creation of new funds and endowments (such as UnLtd and Impetus), networks of support and training (such as CAN - the Community Action Network - and Ashoka), as well as new legal forms (like the UK's Community Interest Company). Foundations are becoming much more sophisticated about their impact on social change and a new generation of philanthropists familiar with innovation in business are looking for more effective ways to invest money in social projects that go beyond the piecemeal paternalism of the past.

Here we aim to build on this progress, by broadening the focus to look at how societies renew themselves not just through social enterprise but also through social innovation more widely in NGOs, the public sector, movements and markets. The main aim is practical – and towards the end of this manifesto we set out the steps that now need to be taken to accelerate social innovation more broadly and meet unmet needs. But we also make the case for better understanding and rigorous reflection in a field that still relies too much on anecdote and inspiring stories.

We see the development of social innovation as an urgent task – one of the most urgent there is. There is a wide, and probably growing, gap between the scale of the problems we face and the scale of the solutions on offer. New methods for advancing social innovation are relevant in every sector but they are likely to offer most in fields where problems are intensifying (from diversity and conflict, to climate change and mental illness), in fields where existing models are failing or stagnant (from traditional electoral democracy to criminal justice), and in fields where new possibilities (such as mobile technologies and open source methods) are not being adequately exploited.

We expected there to be a vast body of literature, research and accumulated wisdom on how social innovation happens. There is certainly no shortage of good writings on innovation in business and technology, from such figures as Everett Rogers, Christopher Freeman, Rosabeth Moss Kanter, William Baumol, Eric Von Hippel, Bart Nooteboom, Clay Christianson and John Kao. Yet there is a remarkable dearth of serious analysis of how social innovation is done and how it can be supported, and in a survey of the field we have found little serious research, no widely shared concepts, thorough histories, comparative research or quantitative analysis.[2]

This neglect is mirrored by the lack of practical attention paid to social innovation. Vast amounts of money are spent by business on innovation to meet both real and imagined consumer demands. Almost as much is spent by governments (much of it to devise new methods of killing people). But far less is spent by governments or NGOs or foundations to more systematically develop innovative solutions to common needs. And not one country has a serious strategy for social innovation that is remotely comparable to the strategies for innovation in business and technology.

The Young Foundation: a centre of past and future social innovation

At the Young Foundation we have particular reasons for being interested in this field. For over 50 years the Young Foundation's precursors were amongst the world's most important centres both for understanding social enterprise and innovation and doing it. They helped create dozens of new institutions (such as the Open University and its parallels around the world, Which?, the School for Social Entrepreneurs and the Economic and Social Research Council) and pioneered new social models (such as phone based health diagnosis, extended schooling and patient led health care). Michael Young was judged by Harvard's Daniel Bell the world's 'most successful entrepreneur of social enterprises', and in his work and his writings he anticipated today's interest in social enterprise and the broader question of how societies innovate.[3]

This tradition of practical social innovation is now being energetically revived from our base in east London. We are working with cities, governments, companies and NGOs to accelerate their capacity to innovate; and we are also launching new organisations and models which can better meet people's needs for care, jobs and homes. This work is mainly motivated by the desire to act – by the principle that if you see a problem your first duty is to try to solve it, rather than simply writing about it or trying to persuade someone else to act. This manifesto sets out some of our thinking. The first part provides an overview of social innovation, its definition, history and key stages. The second part sets out some of the ways that this agenda can be taken forward through research and practical action.

What social innovation is

Defining social innovation

Innovation is often given complex definitions. We prefer the simple one: 'new ideas that work'. This differentiates innovation from improvement (which implies only incremental change); and from creativity and invention (which are vital to innovation but miss out the hard work of implementation and diffusion that makes promising ideas useful). So social innovation refers to new ideas that work in meeting social goals. Defined in this way the term has, potentially, very wide boundaries – from gay partnerships to new ways of using mobile phone texting, and from new lifestyles to new products and services.

Our interest here is in a narrower subset of social innovation: innovations that take the form of replicable programmes or organisations. A good example of a socially innovative *activity* in this sense is the spread of cognitive behavioural therapy, proposed in the 1960s by Aaron Beck, tested empirically in the 1970s, and then spread through professional and policy networks in the subsequent decades. A good example of socially innovative new *organisations* is the Big Issue, and its international successor network of magazines sold by homeless people (and its more recent spin-offs, like the Homeless World Cup competition in which teams of homeless people compete).

We are interested here in innovations that have also changed the balance of power – giving the relatively poor and powerless more control over their own lives and advancing social justice.

A contented and stable world might have little need for innovation. Innovation becomes an imperative when problems are getting worse, when systems aren't working or when institutions reflect past rather than present problems. As the great Victorian historian Lord Macauley wrote: 'there is constant improvement precisely because there is constant discontent'.

Discontent is one driver of innovation. The other is awareness of a gap between what there is and what there ought to be, between what people need and what they are offered by governments, private firms and NGOs.

These are some of the fields where we see particularly severe innovation deficits:

- Ageing populations which require, for example, new ways of organising pensions, care, mutual support, housing, urban design, mobility and new methods of countering isolation.

- The growing diversity of countries and cities which is demanding innovative ways of organising schooling, language training and housing, to avoid the risks of conflict and mutual resentment.

- The rising incidence of chronic diseases including arthritis, depression and diabetes. Some once acute diseases (such as cancers and heart disease) are becoming chronic. It is widely acknowledged that the key solutions will have as much to do with social organisation as with medical provision.

- Many of the behavioural problems that partly result from affluence are getting worse, including obesity, bad diets and inactivity as well as addictions to alcohol, drugs, gambling. None of these is easily addressed by traditional models.

- Difficult transitions to adulthood - how to help teenagers successfully navigate their way into more stable careers, relationships and lifestyles.

- Crime and punishment - in some countries (including the UK) a majority of convicted criminals re-offend within two years of leaving prison, a striking pattern of failure.

- The mismatch between growing GDP and stagnant happiness (and declining real welfare according to some measures).

- The glaring challenges that surround climate change - how to reorder cities, transport systems and housing to dramatically reduce carbon emissions, and how to adapt to climate changes which may already be irreversible.

In each of these fields the dominant existing models simply do not work well enough. Often they are too inflexible and unimaginative. They may be fitted to past problems or bound by powerful interests. They may be provided by agencies that have become complacent or outdated. The result is unnecessary human suffering, and unrealised potential.

A short history of social innovation

Much of what we take for granted in social policy and service delivery began as radical innovation, as promising ideas and unproven possibilities: the idea of a national health service freely available to all was at first seen as absurdly utopian (and has still not been achieved in many big countries, including the USA and China). It was once thought absurd to imagine that ordinary people could be trusted to drive cars at high speed. Often what we now consider common sense was greeted by powerful interest groups with hostility. As Schopenhauer observed, 'every truth passes through three stages. First, it is ridiculed. Second, it is violently opposed. Third, it is accepted as being self-evident.'

Over the last two centuries innumerable social innovations have moved from the margins to the mainstream. They include: the invention and spread of trade unions and cooperatives, which drew on earlier models of guilds but radically reshaped them for the grim factories of 19th century industry; the spread of collective insurance against sickness and poverty, from self-organised communities to states; the spread of new models of the university in the 19th century, which drew on the traditional examples of al-Azhar, Paris and Oxford, but redefined them to meet the needs of modern industrial societies; the spread of the kindergarten, building on Friedrich Froebel's ideas that were embodied in the first kindergarten in 1837; and the spread of sports clubs alongside the global enthusiasm for sports like football and cricket.

During some periods civil society provided most of the impetus for social innovation. The great wave of industrialisation and urbanisation in the 19th century was accompanied by an extraordinary upsurge of social enterprise and innovation: with mutual self-help, microcredit, building societies, cooperatives, trade unions, reading clubs and philanthropic business leaders creating model towns and model schools. In 19th and early 20th century Britain civil society pioneered the most influential new models of childcare (Barnardos), housing (Peabody), community development (the Edwardian settlements) and social care (Rowntree).

During some periods the lead was taken by social movements. The first of these was the anti-slavery movement in late 18th century Britain which pioneered almost all of what we now associate with campaigns: mass membership, demonstrations, petitions, logos and slogans (including, famously: 'Am I not a man and a brother?'). The 1960s and 1970s saw particularly vigorous social movements around ecology, feminism and civil rights which spawned innovations in governments and commercial markets as well as in NGOs. Sometimes particular events sparked off innovation. In the UK, a 1960s television programme on homelessness called 'Cathy Come Home' prompted the creation of the NGO Shelter, and 40 years of innovation in providing shelter and care for people sleeping on streets. Another wave of civic innovation is under way in the 2000s as the power of the internet and global media is harnessed to causes like world poverty and the environment.

At other times governments have taken the lead in social innovation, for example in the years after 1945 when democratic governments built welfare states, schooling systems and institutions as various as credit banks for farmers and networks of adult education colleges (this was a period when many came to see civic and charitable organisations as too parochial, paternalist and inefficient to meet social needs on any scale).

Social innovation has never been restricted to what we would now call social policy. Robert Owen in 19th century Scotland attempted to create an entirely new economy and society in embryo from his base in Lanarkshire. More recently successful innovations have grown up in banking (the bank with one of the world's highest credit ratings, Rabobank, is a cooperative), in multiple industries (Mondragon in Spain is a network of cooperatives that employs some 80,000 people) and in utilities (in the UK one of the most successful privatised utilities is the one that chose to become a mutual - Welsh Water/Glas Cymru). In many countries significant shares of agriculture, retailing, and finance are organised through coops and mutuals that combine economic and social goals. There has also been social innovation in the media: from trade union newspapers in the 19th century through community radio and television networks to new media forms like Ohmynews in South Korea (perhaps the most important new business model in the media in this decade).

Religion, too, has played a role in generating, sustaining and scaling social innovation, from Florence Nightingale (who was supported by nurses from the Irish Sisters of Mercy) to the black faith-inspired pioneer, Mary Seacole, who also set up new medical facilities during the Crimean war, to the Victorian settlements which paved the way for so much 20th century social change. In South Africa the anti-apartheid movement depended greatly on faith, while in the US black churches were the drivers of the civil rights movement and innovations in micro-banking, mutual welfare and even recent adoption strategies. Recent years have also seen the emergence of new waves of engaged Muslim NGOs such as Islamic Relief.

Looking back it is hard to find any field in which social innovation has not played an important role. The spread of the car, for example, depended not just on the technology of the internal combustion engine and modern production lines, but also on a host of associated social innovations: driving schools, road markings and protocols, garages, traffic wardens and speeding tickets, and more recently congestion charging systems.

Improvements in healthcare depended on innovations in medicine (including antibiotics) and surgery (from sterilisation to keyhole surgery) but also on a host of other innovations including: public health systems to provide clean water and sewers; changing home habits to promote cleanliness in kitchens; new methods of measurement (a primary interest of Florence Nightingale who was as innovative a statistician as she was a nurse); new organisational forms such as primary care practices and barefoot health services; new business forms in pharmaceuticals to enable long-term investment in research (for example, Du Pont); state regulation of food to promote safety, and more recently to cut sugar and salt contents; provision of meals to children in schools (which during some periods did more to advance health than any other single measure); national health services funded by taxpayers; self help groups, and civil organisations for diseases such as Alzheimer's; volunteers, trained for example to use defibrillators; and new models of care such as the hospices pioneered by Cicely Saunders. Modern health's heroes are not just the pioneers of new drugs and surgical procedures. They also include social innovators like Edwin Chadwick,[4] whose report on *The Sanitary Conditions of the Labouring Population* (published in 1842 when the average life expectancy for factory workers in the new industrial towns and cities like Bolton in north-west England was only 17 years) successfully persuaded government to provide clean water, sewers, street cleaning and refuse.

Health is typical in this respect. Simplistic accounts in which progress is caused by technology invariably fall apart on closer inspection. Instead most of what we now count as progress has come the mutual reinforcement of social, economic, technological and political innovations.

10 world-changing social innovations

1. The Open University – and the many models of distance learning that have opened up education across the world and are continuing to do so.

2. Fair trade – pioneered in the UK and USA in the 1940s-80s and now growing globally.

3. Greenpeace – and the many movements of ecological direct action which drew on much older Quaker ideas and which have transformed how citizens can engage directly in social change.

4. Grameen – alongside BRAC and others whose new models of village and community based microcredit have been emulated worldwide.

5. Amnesty International – and the growth of human rights.

6. Oxfam (originally the Oxford Committee for Relief of Famine) and the spread of humanitarian relief.

7. The Women's Institute (founded in Canada in the 1890s)– and the innumerable women's organisations and innovations which have made feminism mainstream.

8. Linux software - and other open source methods such as Wikipedia and Ohmynews that are transforming many fields.

9. NHS Direct and the many organisations, ranging from Doctor Robert to the Expert Patients Programme, which have opened up access to health and knowledge about health to ordinary people.

10. Participatory budgeting models – of the kind pioneered in Porto Alegre and now being emulated, alongside a broad range of democratic innovations, all over the world.

Who does social innovation

There are many lenses through which to understand social innovation. For much of the last century it was understood within much broader frameworks for thinking about social change, industrialisation and modernity. Small innovations were seen as reflections of big dynamics. In the contrary approach advocated by Karl Popper and others, social innovation was the incremental and experimental alternative to the errors of utopian blueprints and violent revolution (our reflections on theories of change and their relevance to social innovation are contained in this endnote[5]).

Heroic individuals

Today most discussion of social innovation tends to adopt one of two main lenses for understanding how change happens.

In the first social change is portrayed as having been driven by a very small number of heroic, energetic and impatient individuals. History is told as the story of how they remade the world, persuading and cajoling the lazy and timid majority into change. Robert Owen, Octavia Hill and Michael Young are three people who embody this view of history.

The most important social innovator from the 18th century was arguably Robert Owen, born in 1771 at the dawn of the industrial revolution.[6] By the turn of the century he had bought four textile factories in New Lanark and was determined to use them not just to make money but to remake the world. Arguing that people were naturally good but corrupted by harsh conditions, under Owen's management the cotton mills and village of New Lanark became a model community. When Owen arrived at New Lanark children from as young as five were working for 13 hours a day in the textile mills. He stopped employing children under ten and sent young children to newly built nursery and infant schools, while older children combined work and secondary school. In addition to schools New Lanark set up a crèche for working mothers, free medical care, and comprehensive education, including evening classes. There were concerts, dancing, music-making and pleasant landscaped areas. His ideas inspired emulators all over the world (and New Lanark remains a popular tourist attraction) and he had an enormous influence on the new cooperative and mutualist movements as well as paving the way for modern management theories.

The 19th century produced many more social innovators. A good example is Octavia Hill, who was born in 1838.[7] Her father had been a follower of Robert Owen and as a child she was exposed to an extraordinary range of contemporary progressive thinkers, including Dr. Thomas Southwood Smith, 'father of sanitary reform,' F.D.Maurice, the leader of the Christian Socialists, and John Ruskin. In 1864, Ruskin bought three buildings in Paradise Place, a notorious slum, and gave them to Octavia Hill to manage.

The aim was to make 'lives noble, homes happy, and family life good' and her determination, personality, and skill transformed the poverty-stricken areas into tolerably harmonious communities. Communal amenities such as meeting halls, savings clubs, and dramatic productions were encouraged. Her training programmes laid the foundations of the modern profession of housing management and her first organisation, the Horace Street Trust (now Octavia Housing and Care) became the model for all subsequent housing associations. Octavia Hill was the first advocate of a green belt for London; launched the Army Cadet Force to socialise inner city teenagers; campaigned to create public parks and to decorate hospitals with arts and beauty; and in 1895 created the National Trust (which now has more than 3.4million members), arguably the world's first great modern heritage organisation.

Michael Young (after whom the Young Foundation is named) was one of the 20th century's outstanding social innovators. Born in 1915 his life and work illuminates many of the complexities of the story. As Head of Research for the Labour Party in 1945, he helped shape the welfare state and saw the power of the government to change people's lives, not least through radical social innovations including the National Health Service and comprehensive welfare provision. He became concerned, however, about the risks of government becoming over mighty and moved out to east London to approach change through a very different route. His approach involved argument - and he wrote a series of bestsellers changing attitudes to a host of social issues, including urban planning (leading the movement away from tower blocks), education (leading thinking about how to radically widen access) and poverty. He also pioneered ideas of public and consumer empowerment in private markets and in public services: NHS Direct, the spread of after-school clubs and neighbourhood councils can all be traced to Michael's work. However, for our purposes, his most important skill lay in creating new organisations and models: in total some 60 independent organisations including the Open University, the Consumers' Association, Language Line, Education Extra and the Open College of the Arts. Some of these drew on formal academic research; others simply drew on hunches; and others still drew on informal conversations on buses or street corners which illuminated people's unmet needs.[8]

Although many of these ideas look obvious in retrospect they were generally met with hostility, and one of Michael Young's characteristics (shared with many pioneers in social innovation) was, in the words of one of his collaborators, Tony Flower: 'sheer persistence, a kind of benign ruthlessness, clutching onto an idea beyond the bitter end, always taking no as a question.' Many of his projects began very small – often only one or two people working from a basement in Bethnal Green. But he was always looking for small changes that could achieve leverage by demonstrating how things could work differently. And he was convinced that practical action was often more convincing than eloquent books and pamphlets.

Another striking feature of his work was that he straddled different sectors – as did his creations. Most of them became voluntary organisations. But some which began as voluntary organisations ended up as public bodies (such as the Open University); some which had been conceived as public bodies ended up as voluntary organisations (Which? for example); and some which began as voluntary organisations ended up as for-profit enterprises (like Language Line which was recently sold for £25m).

These individuals are particularly outstanding examples drawn from British history. They combined an ability to communicate complex ideas in compelling ways with a practical ability to make things happen. There are countless other examples of similar social innovators from around the world – and the leaders of social innovation have included politicians, bureaucrats, intellectuals, business people as well as NGO activists. Some are widely celebrated like Muhammad Yunus the founder of Grameen, and Kenyan Nobel Prize winner Wangari Maathai, or Saul Alinsky the inventor of community organising in the USA.

There are also many less well-known but deeply impressive figures (some of whom are described in David Bornstein's book on 'How to Change the World'[9]). These accounts include the stories of: Jeroo Billimoria, founder of the India-wide Childline, a 24-hour helpline and emergency response system for children in distress[10]; Vera Cordeiro, founder of Associacao Saude Crianca Rensacer in Brazil[11]; Taddy Blecher, founder of the Community and Individual Development Association (CIDA) City Campus, the first private higher education institution in South Africa to offer a virtually free business degree to students from disadvantaged backgrounds,[12] and Karen Tse, founder of International Bridges to Justice.

These individual stories are always inspiring, energising, and impressive. They show just how much persistent, dedicated people can achieve against the odds; and they serve as reminders of the courage that always accompanies radical social change.

Social innovation through movements

There is, however, a very different lens through which to understand the question of who drives social innovation. Seen through this lens individuals are the carriers of ideas rather than originators. Detailed study of particular innovations usually shows that many people were involved and that similar ideas sprang up in different places at the same time. The spread of village microcredit, for example, grew in parallel through several organisations in Bangladesh in the 1970s (in particular Grameen and BRAC), as well as in South America, and drew on models that were widespread in 19th century Europe.

If we ask which movements had the most impact over the last half century the role of individuals quickly fades into the background. The far-reaching movements of change, such as feminism or environmentalism, involved millions of people and had dozens of intellectual and organisational leaders, many of whom had the humility to realise that they were often as much following, and channelling, changes in public consciousness as they were standing above them.

Like individual change-makers these movements have their roots in ideas grown from discontent. But their histories look very different. Environmentalism, for example, grew from many different sources. There were precursors in the 19th century, including: movements for protecting forests and landscapes; scientifically inspired movements to protect biodiversity; more politicised movements to counter the pollution of big companies or gain redress for their victims; movements of direct action like Greenpeace (which itself drew on much older Quaker traditions); and the various Green Parties around the world which have always been suspicious of individual leaders. Environmentalism has spawned a huge range of social innovations, from urban recycling to community owned wind farms. Today environmentalism is as much part of big business culture (as companies like BP try to finesse the shift to more renewable energy sources), as it is of the alternative business culture of organic food and household composting, municipal government (for example the many dozens of US Mayors who committed themselves to Kyoto in the early 2000s), and of civil society (through mass campaigns like Friends of the Earth).

Feminism too grew out of many different currents[13]. In the West it had its roots in the humanism of the 18th century and the Industrial Revolution, and in the French Revolution's Women's Republican Club. It evolved as a movement that was simultaneously intellectual and cultural (pushed forward by pioneers like Emmeline Pankhurst, Simone de Beauvoir and Germaine Greer), political (New Zealand was the first country to give all adult women the vote and along with Scandinavia has consistently been ahead of the US, Germany, France and the UK) and economic (helped by women's growing power in the labour market). Many of its ideas were crystallised through legislation: Norway's ruling Labour Party's recent proposal to require big companies to have 40% of their boards made up of women is just one example.

As in the case of environmentalism, thousands of social innovations grew out of the movement: from clubs and networks to promote women in particular professions, to integrated childcare centres, abortion rights, equitable divorce laws and protections against rape and sexual harassment, and maternity leave and skills programmes for mothers returning to the labour market.

Disability rights is another example of a powerful set of ideas whose impact is still being felt on building regulation, employment practices and public policy, as well as on popular culture, as stereotypes that were once acceptable are shown to be degrading and offensive.[14] As recently as 1979 it was legal for some state governments in the USA to sterilize disabled persons against their will. During the 1980s and 1990s the disability movement became increasingly militant: voluntary organisations serving disabled people went through fierce battles as the beneficiaries fought to take control over NGOs that had been established as paternalistic providers for mute recipients. Thanks to their battles, legislation conferred new rights and obligations on employers and planners; and technologists accelerated their efforts to innovate - for example, through the Center for Independent Living founded by disability activists in Berkeley, California 1972 and the development of technologies such as telecaptioners, text telephones, voice-recognition systems, voice synthesizers and screen readers.

All of these movements changed the world and all of them, interestingly, adopted an ethos that was suspicious of overly individualistic pictures of change. In their view the idea that progress comes from the wisdom of a few exceptional individuals is an anachronism, a throwback to pre-democratic times. All of these movements have also emphasised empowerment – enabling people to solve their own problems rather than waiting for the state, or heroic leaders, to solve problems for them.

How social innovation happens: the uneasy symbiosis of 'bees' and 'trees'

Both of these accounts of social innovation – the one focused on individuals the other focused on broader movements – bring with them useful insights. Both call attention to the cultural base for social innovation – the combination of exclusion, resentment, passion and commitment that make social change possible. Both confirm that social innovations also spread in an 'S curve', with an early phase of slow growth amongst a small group of committed supporters, then a phase of rapid take-off, and then a slowing down as saturation and maturity are achieved.

Both accounts also rightly emphasise the importance of ideas – visions of how things could be different and better. Every successful social innovator or movement has succeeded because it has planted the seeds of an idea in many minds. In the long run ideas are more powerful than individuals or institutions; indeed, as John Maynard Keynes noted, 'the world is ruled by little else'.

But neither story is really adequate to explain the complexities of social change. Change rarely happens without some brave people willing to take risks and a stand. Leadership matters even in the most egalitarian and democratic movement. But equally it is the nature of social change that it depends on many people being persuaded to abandon old habits. Even the great religious prophets only spawned great religions because they were followed by great organisers and evangelists and military conquerors who were able to focus their energies and create great organisations.[15]

In what follows we drill down in greater detail to analyse the different stages through which social innovations often emerge and spread, as ideas take concrete form - stages in which both individuals and wider movements sometimes play decisive roles. Later on we use this schema to show which stages are missing or underdeveloped in particular sectors.

At each stage we show that new ideas have to secure support if they are to survive. The support they need may include: the passion and commitment of other people; the money of patrons or a state; and contracts or consumers. Social change depends, in other words, on alliances between what could be called the 'bees' and the 'trees': the bees are the small organisations, individuals and groups who have the new ideas, and are mobile, quick and able to cross-pollinate. The trees are the big organisations – governments, companies or big NGOs – which are poor at creativity but generally good at implementation, and which have the resilience, roots and scale to make things happen. Both need each other.

Generating ideas by understanding needs and identifying potential solutions

The starting point for innovation is some idea of a need that isn't being met and some idea of how it could be met. Sometimes needs are glaringly obvious - like hunger, homelessness or disease. But sometimes needs are less obvious, or not recognised - like the need for protection from domestic violence, or racism, and it takes campaigners and movements to name and describe these.

Needs come to the fore in many ways - through angry individuals and groups, campaigns, political movements as well as through careful observation. They may come from informal social movements (like health related, online self-help groups[16]); religious movements (instrumental in the Jubilee debt campaign); existing voluntary organisations (the RNID leading the move to digital hearing aids); individual social entrepreneurs (Octavia Hill founding the National Trust and pioneering occupational therapy); rising citizen expectations and aspirations (such as patient attitudes towards health professionals resulting in patient choice); or demographic change (Language Line catering for the needs of public services and people for whom English is a second language).

Some of the best innovators spot needs which aren't being adequately met by the market or the state. They are often good at talking and listening, digging below the surface to understand peoples' needs and dislocations, dissatisfactions and blockages. (Michael Young got many of his best ideas from random conversations on street corners, buses and even in cemeteries.) Empathy is the starting point and ethnography is usually a more relevant formal tool than statistical analysis. Personal motivations also play a critical role: people may want to solve their own problems and they may be motivated by the suffering of their friends or family.

Some of the most effective methods for cultivating social innovation start from the presumption that people are competent interpreters of their own lives and competent solvers of their own problems. Anyone seeking to find an answer to the management of chronic diseases or alienation amongst teenagers may do best to find how people are themselves solving their problems. Another method is to find the people who are solving their problems against the odds – the ex-prisoners who do not re-offend or the 18 year old without any qualifications who nevertheless finds a job. Looking for the 'positive deviants' - the approaches that work when most others are failing – gives insights into what might be possible, and usually at much lower cost than top down solutions.

Needs then have to be tied to new possibilities. New possibilities may be technological – for example, using the mobile telephone to support frontline workers, using digital television to strengthen local communities, or using artificial intelligence to guide family law, as in Victoria in Australia. Indeed the internet is now generating a host of new business models that are set to have enormous impact in the social field (some of these are being collected by the Open Business Network, which is linked to the Young Foundation[17]).

Other possibilities may derive from new organisational forms, like the Community Interest Company recently launched in the UK, or the special purpose vehicles increasingly used in global development. Or possibilities may derive from new knowledge - for example, newly acquired understanding of the importance of early years development in shaping future life chances. Innovators generally have a wide peripheral vision – and are good at spotting how apparently unrelated methods and ideas can be used.

Few ideas emerge fully formed. Instead innovators often try things out, and then quickly adjust them in the light of experience. Tinkering seems to play a vital role in all kinds of innovation, involving trial and error, hunches and experiments that only in retrospect look rational and planned.

New social ideas are also rarely inherently new in themselves. More often they combine ideas that had previously been separate. Examples of creative combinations include diagnostic health lines (which combined the telephone, nurses and diagnostic software); magazines sold by homeless people; the linking of gay rights to marriage; applying the idea of rights to animals; or the use of swipe cards to make possible large scale bicycle hiring schemes, located in stations or next to bus shelters. Many of the most important ideas straddle the boundaries between sectors and disciplines (about 50% of public sector innovation is now reckoned to cross organisational boundaries, for example).

Some organisations use formal creativity methods to generate possibilities, including the ones devised by Edward de Bono[18], the design company Ideo, and the consultancy What If?, all of which aim to free groups to think more laterally, and to spot new patterns. Some of these methods force creativity - for example, getting developers and designers to engage with the toughest customers, or those facing the most serious problems, to force more lateral solutions.

Creativity can be stimulated by other peoples' ideas which are increasingly being collected and banked. Nicholas Albery, a regular collaborator with Michael Young, founded the Institute for Social Inventions in 1985, produced regular editions of the Book of Social Inventions and the Book of Visions, and, in 1995, helped launch the Global Ideas Bank – a rich online source of ideas and experiences (which also produces regular editions of the Global Ideas Book).[19]

In some cases ideas can be bought on the open market. The company Innocentive, for example, offers cash rewards on the web for innovators who have workable solutions to problems they solve, based on an assumption that often in a neighbouring sector a similar structure of problem may already have been solved. There are also now many innovation labs, some linked to universities, some linked to companies and some focused on particular problems, including the MIT Community Innovation Lab, the Social Action Laboratory at Melbourne and the Affirmative Action Laboratory in South Africa.[20]

All societies throw up many possible social innovations. Some never get beyond a conversation in a kitchen or a bar. Many briefly take organisational form but then fade as enthusiasm dims or it becomes obvious that the idea isn't so good after all. But the key to success is to ensure that there is as wide as possible a range of choices to draw on. As Linus Pauling (who won Nobel prizes in chemistry and peace) observed, 'the way to get good ideas is to get lots of ideas and throw the bad ones away.'

Developing, prototyping and piloting ideas

The second phase of any innovation process involves taking a promising idea and testing it out in practice. Few plans survive their first encounter with reality. But it is through action that they evolve and improve. Social innovations may be helped by formal market research or desk analysis but progress is often achieved more quickly through turning the idea into a prototype or pilot and then galvanising enthusiasm.

Social innovations are often implemented early. Because those involved are usually highly motivated they are too impatient to wait for governments or professions. The experience of trying to make them work then speeds up their evolution, and the power of example then turns out to be as persuasive as written argument or advocacy. Michael Young, for example, usually moved very quickly to set up an embryonic organisation rather than waiting for detailed business plans and analyses.

The Language Line organisation, for example, began as two people with telephones and a tiny contract with the neighbouring police station.

A key virtue of quick prototyping is that innovations often require several goes before they work. The first outings are invariably flawed. The NHS took 40 years to move from impossible dream to reality; the radio took a decade to find its form (its early pioneers wrongly assumed that members of the public would purchase airtime to send messages to their friends and families, as with the telephone); what became Wikipedia was a failure in its first outing.

There is now a much richer range of methods available for prototyping, piloting and testing new ideas either in real environments or in protected conditions, halfway between the real world and the laboratory. The relatively free money of foundations and philanthropists can be decisive in helping ideas through this phase. Governments have also become more sophisticated in their use of evidence and knowledge,[21] with a proliferation of pilots, pathfinders and experiments. Incubators, which have long been widespread in business, have started to take off in the public sector and amongst NGOs, though practice and understanding remains very patchy. In business new devices like 3D printers have made it easier to turn ideas quickly into prototypes – in the social field parallel methods are being developed to crystallise promising ideas so that they can be quickly tested.

Some ideas that seem good on paper fall at this stage. Michael Young for example launched a DIY garage convinced that most motorists would prefer to invest some of their time in exchange for lower costs. They didn't.[22] But even failed ideas often point the way to related ideas that will succeed. As Samuel Beckett put it: 'Try Again. Fail again. Fail better.'

Assessing then scaling up and diffusing the good ones

The third stage of the social innovation process comes when an idea is proving itself in practice and can then be grown, potentially through organic growth, replication, adaptation or franchising.

Taking a good idea to scale requires skilful strategy and coherent vision, combined with the ability to marshal resources and support and identify the key points of leverage, the weak chinks in opponents' walls. 'Bees' need to find supportive 'trees' with the machineries to make things happen on a big scale. That in turn may demand formal methods to persuade potential backers, including investment appraisals, impact assessments and newer devices to judge success like 'social returns on investment' or 'blended value'.

Communication is essential at this stage – social innovators need to capture the imagination of a community of supporters through the combination of contagious courage and pragmatic persistence. Good names, along with brands, identities and stories play a critical role. Some social innovations then spread through the organic growth of the organisations that conceived them – like the Samaritans volunteer service providing confidential, emotional support. Some have grown through federations – including many NGOs like Age Concern or the Citizens Advice Bureaux. Governments have often played the critical role in scaling up social innovations and have unique capacities to do this by: passing laws (many social movements have achieved their greatest impact by persuading parliaments to pass new laws, for example giving women the vote, or legalising gay marriage); committing spending (for example, to extended schools); and conferring authority on public agencies (for example, to grow the role of health visitors). Business grows ideas through a well-established range of methods some of which are becoming more commonly used in the social sector including: organic growth of an originating organisation; franchising and licensing; and takeover of similar but less effective organisations

This growth phase is potentially becoming much faster. With the help of the web innovations can spread very quickly, and indeed there can be little point in doing local pilots since the economics of the web may make it as cheap to launch on a national or continental scale. Marginal costs close to zero accelerate the growth phase – but also the phase of decline and disappearance.

A Young Foundation project on scaling up has shown why it is so hard for social innovation to replicate (and pointed to more effective strategies for handling scale). Two necessary conditions are a propitious environment (for example, a market for the service on offer, or government interest in providing funding or contracts) and organisational capacity to grow. These are rare with social innovations. It may take decades to create the environmental conditions for growth – persuading consumers and public agencies to pay for something new. The organisational challenges are no less severe.

In charities and social enterprises the founders who were just right for the organisation during its early years are unlikely to have the right mix of skills and attitudes for a period of growth and consolidation (this is also one of the ways in which an over-individualistic model of change may have become an impediment to the field). Often founders cling on too long - and trustees, funders and stakeholders do not impose necessary changes. By comparison in business the early phases of fast growing enterprises often involve ruthless turnover of managers and executives. Indeed growth in all sectors nearly always involves *outgrowing* founders. Wise founders therefore put in place robust succession plans (and very few successfully remain in executive roles for much more than a decade). Similar considerations apply to organisations which create other organisations. Christian Aid, CAFOD and Tearfund, for example, are all social innovations with global reach today that outgrew their founders and founding institutions (the British Council of Churches, the Catholic Womens' League and the Evangelical Alliance respectively).

In business, the experience of companies such as Microsoft, Procter & Gamble and Amazon suggests that pioneers who create markets through radical innovation are almost never the companies that go on to scale up and dominate them. The skills and mind-sets required for creating a radically new market not only differ from, but actively conflict with, those needed to grow and consolidate. Big companies are often better placed to take new ideas from niche markets to mass markets, and many have concluded that they should subcontract the creation of new and radical products to start-up firms and concentrate their own efforts on consolidating markets, buying up companies or licenses that they see as promising.[23]

For innovators themselves one of the key lessons from all sectors is that ideas spread more quickly when credit is shared, and when at least some of the 'trees' can claim ownership. As President Truman suggested: 'it is amazing what you can achieve if you don't care who gets the credit.'

Learning and evolving

In a fourth stage innovations continue to change: learning and adaptation turns the ideas into forms that may be very different from the expectations of the pioneers. Experience may show unintended consequences, or unexpected applications. In professions, in competitive markets and in the public sector, there is an increasingly sophisticated understanding of how learning takes place. New models such as the collaboratives in health (used by the NHS to improve innovation and practice in fields like cancer and primary care) and closed research groups (used, for example, by a number of major cities to analyse their transport strategies) have helped to embed innovation and improvement into fairly conservative professions.

These highlight the degree to which all processes of innovation can be understood as types of learning, rather than as 'eureka' moments of lone geniuses. Instead, ideas start off as possibilities that are only incompletely understood by their inventors. They evolve by becoming more explicit and more formalised, as best practice is worked out, and as organisations develop experience about how to make them work. This phase involves consolidation around a few core principles which can be easily communicated. Then as the idea is implemented in new contexts it evolves further, and in new combinations, with the learning once again more tacit, held within organisations, until another set of simpler syntheses emerge.

Some organisations appear particularly good at maintaining the momentum from innovation rather than being stuck in a particular form or market. For example the Samaritans in Australia have become a provider of welfare services; the ECT Group in the UK started as a community transport organisation and evolved into a major supplier of kerbside recycling service and is now moving into health. Generally, bigger organisations have more 'absorptive capacity' to learn and evolve - but small ones can gain some of this ability through the skills of their staff and through taking part in the right kinds of networks.

Where social innovation happens

This linear account of innovation provides a useful framework for thinking about change. But it should already be clear that the stages are not always consecutive. Sometimes action precedes understanding. Sometimes doing things catalyses the ideas. There are also feedback loops between every stage, which make real innovations more like multiple spirals than straight lines. These patterns also manifest themselves differently in different sectors. Real life innovation is a discovery process that often leaves ideas transformed and mutated, and sometimes sees them jump from one sector to another. So, for example, innovations to reduce obesity can be found in public health programmes funded by taxpayers, in self-help groups and in large commercial organisations like Weightwatchers. But each sector does have some distinct patterns, drivers and inhibitors and understanding these is vital for anyone wanting to promote new ideas.

Social organisations and enterprises

In social organisations (charities, community groups, NGOs) new ideas often begin from a particular individual or community's problems or passions. The new model is launched in prototype in a very precarious form before securing resources and support from philanthropists or small donors. Growing new social models usually takes longer than in the other sectors because of the need to align a more complex set of allies and a more complex economic base, though the most successful can in time replicate themselves through growth or emulation. Good examples include the Grameen Bank and BRAC in Bangladesh, The Big Issue and Teach First, or Barnardos Australia's case management systems for children[24]. Community Land Banks are another example, which were pioneered in India, spread to the USA and are now being adopted globally. The web is also making it possible to create new social organisations much more quickly. Pledgebank launched by mySociety.org (led by Young Foundation fellow Tom Steinberg) has created a very powerful tool for bringing groups together to advance a cause. New sources of finance for social enterprise (such as UnLtd) are making it easier for individuals with a good idea to get started, and easier for existing organisations to grow (for example through the loan finance provided by Charity Bank). There is also a small, but growing, group of organisations dedicated to encouraging innovation in the voluntary sector (including the Community Action Network, the Centre for Innovation in Voluntary Action and NFP Synergy).

Table 1: social innovation in social organisations

Generation of possibilities	Prototypes	Growth
Practice, imagination, beneficiaries and user inputs generate possibilities.	Start ups, incubators, learning by doing and pilots road test ideas (for example, Pledgebank, new models of refugee integration).	Organisational growth, emulation, replication and franchise to achieve scale (for example, Medecins Sans Frontieres, Wikipedia, Grameen, Teach First).

Social movements

Social movements operate in the space between politics and civil society. To succeed they have to address a compelling fear or aspiration. Generally speaking, innovative social movements start out with small groups seeking likeminded allies, animated by anger or hope. They then develop into more organized campaigns that try to demonstrate the four key attributes of any successful social movement: worthiness, unity, numbers and commitment. States can play a decisive role in helping them to succeed – or blocking them. Campaigns for equal opportunities, for example, moved from the radical margins in the 1960s to transform mainstream business, helped along the way by legislation. More recent examples of innovative campaigns include Make Poverty History, a dramatically novel kind of campaign linking politicians and celebrities, and the Fathers for Justice campaign, which made headlines with its use of shock tactics in advocating fathers' rights.

Table 2: social innovation in social movements

Formation	Campaigning and advocacy	Legislation, habit change, changed values
Small groups, seeking likeminded allies, spurred by anger, resentment (for example, current campaigns against slavery or for legalised prostitution).	Movements try to demonstrate worthiness, unity, numbers and commitment (for example, slow food, Fathers4Justice, ONE and Make Poverty History).	Governments endorse claims and pass legislation (for example, equal opportunities in business, gay marriage). Public habits change.

Politics and government

Politicians and political activists promote new ideas partly to promote their beliefs and partly to gain an edge in political competition – more public support and more chance of winning and retaining power. They campaign through party structures, newspaper articles, meetings and lobbies to get their ideas into party programmes and manifestos, ministerial speeches and programmes, and then into legislation or spending programmes. For example, campaigns for tougher building regulations requiring energy efficient materials, support for community bus services and foyers for homeless teenagers all focused on politics as the best route to achieve change, even if the services were then run by NGOs.

Some political leaders are natural social innovators: Jaime Lerner, mayor of Curitiba in Brazil, has, over several decades, been an outstanding example completely refashioning his city's transport system, rebuilding parks and libraries and experimenting with lateral solutions, such as paying slum children for bringing rubbish out of slums with vouchers for transport. Some political leaders take pride in being on the cutting edge of cultural and social change: the City of San Francisco, for example, pays for sex change operations as a result of politics, while in the 1980s Ken Livingstone's London pioneered radical models of equal opportunity, appropriate technology and social inclusion that were well ahead of mainstream voluntary organisations.

Table 3: social innovation in politics

Demands and campaigns	Policy formulation and manifestos	Public spending, programmes Legislation, new professions
NGOs, party activists, people in need and the media make demands for new programmes (such as father's rights, or free eldercare).	Politicians become champions, ministers and officials take up issues and give political commitment (for example, to extended schools or new powers for neighbourhood governance).	Bureaucrats and professionals then implement, provide funding and authority (for example, for tax credits, early years centers or bicycle transport networks).

Within government bureaucracies there is rather a different story of social innovations gaining momentum, away from the glare of party politics. The motivation is usually to address a compelling problem or to cut costs. Here the experience of officials themselves, consultations and contestable markets can be key to taking innovations from ideas into reality. Promising ideas may be tested through incubators (like Singapore's incubator for e-government ideas), or zones (like the UK's Employment Zones), pathfinders or pilots, with formal assessment and evaluation methods to prove their efficacy.

Scaling up is then achieved through new structures and spending programmes. A good example of encouraging public innovation is the partnership between the state and city of New York to support the Centre for Court Innovation which helps develop, test out and appraise new approaches to courts and crime reduction introducing, for example, specialist drug and domestic violence courts.

Table 4: social innovation in government

Generation of possibilities	Piloting, testing, learning by doing	Scaling up
Creativity methods, consultations, contestability and the adaptation of models from other sectors generate possibilities (for example, weekend prisons or nurse led primary care).	Incubators, zones, and pathfinders – with assessment and evaluation methods – test and capture lessons (for example, restorative justice or carbon markets, or uses of artificial intelligence in family law).	Growth, new structures, franchises and spending programmes achieve scale (for example, urban road charging and integrated web portals).

Markets

Commercial markets can also be an effective route for promoting new social ideas. Successive social innovations have gone from the margins of the counterculture into the mainstream using commercial markets. They have generally started with enthusiasts producing and consuming in what is almost a gift economy; then as markets grow enthusiasts are able to form small companies within their own niches, helped by consumers and in some cases by mission-related investment. At a later stage more mainstream investors have often come in, convinced that there really is scope for making profits. Then, in a final stage, what was once marginal becomes mainstream as larger companies try to take models over, making use of their scale, logistical and marketing prowess.

Examples include the evolution of fair trade from being a radical campaign supported by churches and trade unions to the mainstream of most supermarkets. The point at which mainstreaming occurs can be experienced as deeply ambiguous (Nestlé's launch of a range of fair trade products in 2005 being a good example). Another example is the spread of Linux open source software which has, in barely a decade, moved from the margins of computer culture into becoming a dominant technology underpinning the internet and an increasingly powerful competitor to Microsoft. The University of Phoenix is an interesting example of an innovation that took some elements from NGOs and the public sector (including the Open University) and turned them into a successful commercial model that could be quickly scaled up.

There are also many important social innovations in markets themselves. These include innovative types of business organisation (like Denmark's Mandag Morgen, which combines a newsletter, think-tank, forum and consultancy); and new types of market (like the various guaranteed electronic market concepts which are now being piloted in east London). [25]

A small number of companies have pioneered social change rather than following it. The Body Shop is the outstanding example of integrating a social mission with a business one. Business Corporate Social Responsibility is usually more detached from core business activities. However, well designed CSR projects can encourage genuinely radical approaches, and apply imaginative business thinking to social problems. Companies like BP, TNT and Salesforce have given a very high priority to CSR, employee volunteering and creative ways of using corporate resources. But despite the major contribution of business skills to the social sector surprisingly few CSR projects have had a profound influence on the big systems of health, education or welfare. One reason may be that the aim of making projects attractive in reputational terms leads some CSR projects to be gold-plated, which in turn makes them too expensive to be replicated by cash-strapped public sectors. The most useful forms of innovative CSR are more closely tied to core business activities, and therefore considered in terms of direct impacts on profitability, rather than the indirect effects of reputation.

Table 5: social innovation in markets

Embryonic niches	Niche markets	Co-option into mainstream
Enthusiasts produce and consume in what is almost a gift economy (for example, life coaches).	Small companies, mission related investment and consumer and shareholder activism develop niche markets (for example, speed dating or plug in cars).	Multinationals and majors buy in and achieve marketing clout (for example, Linux software, complementary medicine and fair trade).

76332

Academia

New models are sometimes developed in universities, argued about within academic disciplines, put into practice and then evaluated, before spreading. To succeed they have to offer the prospects of peer recognition and to mobilise intellectual labour - for example, from PhD students. Examples include: the Cognitive Behavioural Therapy models used by Martin Seligman to help teenagers avoid depression; models of participant action used to empower communities; the idea of 'food miles', which has led to new thinking about local sourcing; the idea of carbon trading markets; or the work led by Paul Farmer out of Harvard Medical School which led to Partners In Health and the design of new models of community intervention for TB in Haiti which have been adopted by the World Health Organisation. But academia still lacks good mechanisms for cultivating good ideas. After two decades of energetic reform to improve technology transfer universities are only just beginning to think about how to achieve equivalent results in the social field, for example through employing heads of social innovation and social transfer, running social laboratories or incubators to connect users and innovators, or 'social science parks'.

Table 6: social innovation in academia

Invention	Diffusion	Incorporation
New ideas are developed on the margins of academia (for example, 150 year life expectancy).	Ideas are tested in practice or spread through academic networks (for example, Cognitive Behavioural Therapy or participant action).	The once radical idea becomes mainstream (for example, the idea of educating for multiple intelligences).

Philanthropy

Philanthropists are well placed to support innovation: they have money, can often access powerful networks and have the advantage of minimal accountability. In the 19th century philanthropists played an important role in innovation, notably in creating model towns for their workers. In the 20th century the great legacies left by Carnegie, Rockefeller and Ford helped to fund, and shape, creative new approaches to poverty, healthcare and learning (Michael Young's work, for example, was supported by the Ford Foundation).

During much of the 20th century there was very widespread criticism of philanthropy. Its mix of paternalism, idiosyncratic funding and power without accountability were seen as anachronisms. This prompted the more progressive foundations – including Ford in the US and the Rowntree organisations in the UK – to adopt much more radical approaches to empowerment. Today, although many philanthropists continue to support projects in a scattergun way and without much coherent view of social change, a new generation of foundations and individual philanthropists is becoming interested both in social justice and in innovation. The Gates Foundation has been the pre-eminent example in recent years, supporting existing healthcare and poverty alleviation models but also supporting innovation, for example by designing funding tools to incentivise new vaccines and treatments for AIDs, TB and malaria. The sheer scale of resources at its disposal has also enabled it to take a more rounded approach to changing public attitudes and to collaboration with governments. In the UK, Peter Lampl (through the Sutton Trust) has been an outstanding recent example of modern individual philanthropy, with his single minded focus on a specific issue (raising social mobility through education) and his success in combining funding for innovative projects and pilots with support for research and direct influence on public policy.

Common patterns of success and failure

Social innovation doesn't always happen easily, even though people are naturally inventive and curious. In some societies social innovations are strangled at birth, particularly societies where power is tightly monopolized, where free communication is inhibited, or where there are no independent sources of money. Some innovations may simply be too radical to be viable and the phrase 'Leonardo effect' is sometimes used to describe ideas like the helicopter that were too far ahead of the prevailing levels of technology. (By contrast, some of Leonardo da Vinci's other ideas, like flying men with wings attached to their arms or legs simply failed the laws of physics.)

Generally, social innovation is much more likely to happen when the right background conditions are present. For social movements, basic legal protections and status, plus open media and the web are key. In business social innovation can be driven by competition, open cultures and accessible capital, and will be impeded where capital is monopolised by urban elites or government. In politics and government the conditions are likely to include competing parties, think tanks, innovation funds, contestable markets and plentiful pilots. In social organisations the acceleration of social innovation is aided by practitioner networks, allies in politics, strong civic organisations (from trade unions to hospitals) and the support of progressive foundations and philanthropists. And in all of these fields global links make it much easier to learn lessons and share ideas at an early stage, with ideas moving in every direction (for example, the movement of restorative justice from Maori New Zealand to mainstream practice around the world).

Most innovations in business and technology fail. So do most social innovations. Sometimes there are good reasons for failure. An idea may be too expensive; not good enough relative to the alternatives; or flawed by unforeseen side-effects. But we think that many ideas are failing not because of inherent flaws but because of the lack of adequate mechanisms to promote them, adapt them and then scale them up. In business there is a reasonable flow of good innovations in part because of the pull of competitive markets, but also because of public subsidy of technology, and private investment in incubators, venture capital and start-ups. The equivalent potential supports for social innovation – foundations, public agencies – are much weaker. Governments – which typically provide some 40% of NGO finance in countries like the US, Germany, UK, France and Japan - are generally poor at recognising and replicating good innovations, particularly when these come from other sectors. It is notoriously difficult for government to close even failing programmes and services, and there are few incentives for either politicians or officials to take up new ideas. Failure to adapt is rarely career threatening, and anyone who does promote innovations risks upsetting powerful vested interests. It's all too easy to conclude that the apparently promising new idea is too dependent on particular circumstances – such as a charismatic individual – or that the evidence just isn't strong enough (the threshold for evidence on existing programmes tends to be much lower).

Sometimes, too, innovation on the ground may be impeded by structures and systems (and anyone concerned with social change needs to be clear about whether most can be achieved upstream, in the realm of law, policy and structures, or downstream in the practical methods used on the frontline).

Social innovators generally find governments unresponsive. But there are sometimes good reasons for public sectors to be cautious about innovation. Innovation must involve failure – and appetites for failure are bound to be limited in very accountable organisations, or where peoples' lives depend on reliability (for example around traffic light systems, or benefits payments). Most public services, like most NGO service delivery, have to concentrate primarily on better management and performance of existing models rather than invention of new ones.

Innovation is therefore easier where the risks are contained; where there is evident failure; where users have choice (so that they can choose a radically different model of school or doctor rather than having it forced on them); and where expectations are carefully managed (for example through politicians being open to the fact that many models are being tried out and that some are likely to fail). More generally, innovation is likely to be easier when contracts for services reward outcomes achieved rather than outputs or activities, or when there is some competition or contestability rather than monopoly provision by the state. How public sectors 'dock' with the social or non-profit sector is also important here, particularly given that public funding tends to overshadow other revenue sources for many innovations. Funding outcomes rather than activities helps; so too does funding directed to genuinely risk-taking ideas, experiments and trial. Yet we are not aware of a single government that has developed a fully-fledged machinery for accelerating social innovation in a major sector.

Public bodies usually move too slowly for impatient entrepreneurs and activists. But in one important respect they typically move too fast: far-reaching restructurings tend to be driven through much too quickly, ignoring the long time it takes to establish new cultures, procedures and skills, let alone new patterns of trust. For these sorts of systemic change timescales of 10-15 years are more realistic than the shorter timescales of impatient ministers.

The universal story of social innovation

We have suggested some common patterns in social innovation that apply to very diverse examples. Here we want to show how the stories of innovation are similar to stories of change in other fields – such as literature, politics or religion (stories which are summarised in Joseph Campbell's famous book 'The Hero with a Thousand Faces' which attempted to provide a synthesis of many of the world's greatest myths and legends and also provided the inspiration for the Star Wars series). These stories can apply to the lives of individual campaigners and social entrepreneurs; to teams and networks; or even to the ideas themselves as they gain new adherents.

The stories begin with a call or a rejection, a motivating moment which takes the individual out of their routine life and gives them a new mission (for example, Jean Henri Dunant seeing the carnage after the battle of Solferino which later led him to set up the Red Cross or Archbishop Oscar Romero's engagement in human rights after the murder of his friend Rutilio Grande). There is then a long period of travel and adventure as they seek answers or treasures, usually encountering setbacks and rejections, and struggles with dark forces, through which the hero becomes stronger. Finally, there is victory and return when the people who had been rejected or excluded gain what's rightfully theirs and restore the moral order.

These common stories – which apply as much to figures like Mahatma Gandhi and Nelson Mandela as they do to social pioneers – help to explain the waves of dejection, exhilaration and fear that often accompany real social innovations.

They serve as a reminder that good new ideas always have plenty of enemies. All new innovations are in some respects insurgents, threatening to incumbents and therefore likely to be resisted (some times incumbents simultaneously claim that they are already doing the new idea and that it won't work). It has even been said that innovations are sometimes rather like viruses, and that existing organisations and interests act like creatures deploying antibodies to destroy them. The ones that succeed find supporters, alliances, and proponents able to use guile to circumvent barriers. [26]

This overall story also confirms that the most successful social innovators learn to operate in very different landscapes (the heroes in the story pass through mountains, marshes and deserts). In our language here they can thrive across different sectors and know how to exploit their rhythms and cultures. We've already mentioned Michael Young's ability to do this. More recent examples would include Jamie Oliver's campaign to change school dinners which combined the development of media awareness before the broadcast of programmes on Channel 4, followed by a petition of 250,000 people, a demonstration project in Greenwich and astute lobbying of government (all alongside a social enterprise restaurant and a highly profitable sideline in commercial marketing).

Bono in establishing the 'One' campaign in the USA combined celebrity, culture, access to government, and influence in the music business to create a new kind of social movement, which then led to the 'Red' branding exercise.

The hero stories also show how powerless heroes are helped by powerful guides and guardians. In the same way social innovation is rarely either wholly bottom up or wholly top down. The poor and marginalized rarely have access to sufficient resources – financial, political or cultural, to take ideas to scale. The rich and powerful are rarely sufficiently attuned to social need or sufficiently motivated to drive change. The great majority of successful social innovations have therefore involved alliances of the powerful and powerless – for example professionals and graduates working with marginalized communities.

Why we need to know more about social innovation

The observations set out above have been drawn from many case studies, analyses and from our own experience. But we are acutely aware just how much is *not* known about social innovation. In this section we compare what's known about innovation in science and business, and identify the relevant knowledge in surrounding fields which is likely to provide useful insights as the field develops.

What's known about innovation in business and science

The study of innovation in business and science (and to a lesser extent public services) has progressed rapidly over the last few decades, with much richer theories and much more empirical analysis of specific sectors which has yielded a great wealth of insight.[27]

In science, there are distinct literatures on invention and innovation. The research has tried to understand how the substantial public funding that is devoted to basic science should best be used. It has looked at whether to organise funding strategically or reactively in response to scientists' interests and enthusiasms. It has concerned itself with the role of intellectual property protection – and whether, for example, promising biotech ideas in a university should be quickly handed over to private companies and made secret. It has studied the global collaborations that now drive progress in fields like fusion technologies for energy, or new drugs for cancer, and the practical question of how far public support should spread from basic research, through support for generic technologies, to subsidy for promising applications.

In business, the vast volume of analysis done on innovation has given rise to fairly well accepted typologies to understand the different types of innovation connected to products, services and processes. Some have used the distinctions between total, expansionary or evolutionary innovations;[28] others have preferred to differentiate between incremental, radical or systematic ones,[29] or between innovations that happen within organisations and those that cross organisational boundaries.[30]

This body of work has also provided some useful insights.[31] Economists have shown the importance of incentives and returns (including temporary monopolies) and the dynamics whereby many competing innovations consolidate on a dominant model – because of economies of scale, and sometimes because of the power of leading companies.[32] They have also shown the importance of smallness in invention: patents from small firms are twice as likely to be amongst the top 1% of patents subsequently identified as having high impact. Other insights emphasise the importance of abundant venture capital[33] and the common ways in which new models often start on the periphery and are then taken over by big organisations (for example, self service supermarkets began in small retailers before being copied by big ones). Here, once again, we see how 'bees' and 'trees' can complement each other.

Thanks to decades of research we now know that one reason why some sectors have historically been more innovative than others is the role of intermediaries who help make markets work more efficiently, spotting connections and opportunities.[34] More generally, the detailed study of innovation has put an increasing emphasis on the value of relationships rather than formal stocks of knowledge or assets.

Some of the more recent work on the experience of innovation has shown that it is more like a cultural activity than traditional science. The key is often a creative reinterpretation of old problems or solutions by a group of innovators, and it is only by persuading others of this reinterpretation that innovations win support.[35]

One of the reasons that rigorous research into business innovation has proved valuable is that many findings are counterintuitive. For example, in some sectors the best market structure for innovation seems to be a combination of oligopolistic competition between a few big companies and a much larger penumbra of smaller firms (the model that exists in sectors such as microchips, software, cars and retailing). We know that disaggregated industries tend to adapt better to volatility, big structures better to stable conditions. And we know how serendipitous innovation often is – seeking one solution, firms stumble on another, quite different one.

Much of the academic work on innovation has focused on how ideas diffuse, yielding insights into the role of (amongst others) leadership, networks and social systems in determining the likelihood and rate of diffusion.[36] Everett's Rogers's seminal work on diffusion, for example, showed that adopters of any new innovation or idea could be categorized as innovators (2.5%), early adopters (13.5%), early majority (34%), late majority (34%) and laggards (16%), and roughly fitted a Bell Curve. People could fall into different categories for different innovations – so a farmer might be an early adopter of hybrid corn, but a late majority adopter of video recorders. Rogers showed these innovations would spread through society in an 'S' curve, starting off slowly, then spreading much more rapidly until saturation is reached (and he applied his approach not just to business but also to practical health problems, including hygiene, family planning, cancer prevention and drink driving).

Another important issue that has been much studied is the nature of learning between organisations and individuals. For example, one finding is that the most important value of patents is often not their direct impact on production but their role in facilitating learning by increasing the attractiveness of the patent holder as a partner for others.[37]

There is also an extensive literature and body of practice on how innovation should be organised within organisations, pioneered by figures including Peter Drucker, Rosabeth Moss Kanter[38] and John Kao.[39] They have studied the many methods used to generate ideas – pulling in possibilities from sales forces, customers, staff and universities and using skunk works, internal venture funds and competitions or competing teams.

They have also analysed how many ideas are then whittled down to the much smaller proportion that can be financed (the metaphor often used is of a funnel), and then how these can be developed either in house or by turning new ideas into separate businesses run by 'intrapreneurs'.

One finding is that funding that backs groups or individuals rather than specific projects over periods of time may deliver greater results than overly planned innovation.[40] There is also a growing literature on innovation in management practices and organisation[41] and some cases of non-profit sector innovation influencing the business sector.[42] One recent report suggested that innovation in management practices was now more important than product innovation – and that the lead in this field has passed to China.[43] Another rising theme is the important role that users can play in innovation. This has always been mainstream in the social field, but is being given increasing prominence in business – for example by Eric von Hippel and Charles Leadbeater – along with the development of new ways of tying consumers and users into the design of new products and services.[44]

Many of the issues that are thrown up from this work are directly relevant to social innovation. For example, in business there has long been talk of the 'chasm' that innovations have to cross as they pass from being promising pilot ideas to becoming mainstream products or services. There are likely to be quite long phases when revenues are negative, and when investors have to hold their nerve. Exactly the same challenge faces any social innovation. Several methods have been designed to speed up this period, including faster prototyping, intensive handholding by venture capital companies and the use of rigorous milestones against which funds are released – but there is no avoiding a period of uncertainty while success is uncertain (and as Rosabeth Moss Kanter memorably put it, every success looks like a failure in the middle).

The organisational choices faced by social and commercial organisations also run in parallel. Some companies organise innovation largely in-house as part of their mainstream business (like 3M); some create semi-autonomous corporate venture units (like Nokia); some grow through acquisition of other innovative companies as well as their own innovation (Cisco for example); others use widespread networks (like the Original Design Manufacturing companies in China). Again, in the social field there are advantages and disadvantages in keeping innovation in-house (as, for example in the National Health Service in the past); integrating innovative NGOs into big public systems (as has often happened in housing); or using networks (the traditional method of innovation in fields as diverse as public health and urban planning).

In the late 1990s it was briefly fashionable to claim that the whole paradigm of innovation in both business and civil society was being transformed by the internet. In retrospect these claims were greatly overblown. But there is no doubt that the internet both grew out of radically different models and has made new business models possible. Many of the internet's key business innovations emerged from very open processes, without any role for intellectual property: the original technologies of the internet (like the TCP/IP protocol) were developed by networks of programmers supported by the Defense Advanced Research Projects Agency and the Pentagon; and the first web browser was developed at the University of Illinois without any ownership.

More recently, the open source Linux software has grown through a loose community of programmers with few obvious precedents. (For a thorough analysis of open source methods and their great potential see the Young Foundation/Demos publication in 2005: *Wide Open*.[45]). The internet more generally has fostered some very novel business models (from Friends Reunited to the many innovations of Google).

So a lot is known about business innovation. But there are still some fundamental uncertainties; despite the extensive literature and the many departments in universities and business schools this field is far from being a settled science. For example, the debate about intellectual property remains deeply contentious. It used to be thought that property rights were vital to stimulate innovation, and that their absence was one reason why public sectors and NGOs were less innovative than private firms. But there are now plenty of sceptics who point out that most fundamental innovations were not protected as patents. They point out that patents may crush innovation in fields like software and that patents for business ideas (like Amazon's protection of its One-Click purchasing system) reward innovation rather than encouraging it. It has even been suggested that the great majority of universities which have invested in trying to capture the intellectual property they produce have lost money by doing so. [46]

Similarly there is considerable disagreement about the precise role of entrepreneurs – whether, as in Schumpeter's account, they are an elite who drive change, or whether they are better understood as reacting to changes in the environment. There is also disagreement on the precise relationships between market structures and innovation; on the relative virtues of private ownership and public listings on stock exchanges (with some suggesting that privately owned companies are better placed to invest long-term in innovation); and on the appropriate timescales for intellectual property protection.

Business innovation and social innovation: similarities and differences

If the literature on business innovation is extensive but still unsettled the systematic analysis of social innovation barely exists. As we've already seen, some of the patterns may be similar. Social innovations only thrive if they really do meet needs: to spread they need to gain the support of people with resources – funders, investors, purchasers. As in the private sector there will be parallel questions of risk and reward, and of how to manage portfolios of ideas. And equally, again as in the private sector, very capital intensive innovations (the hugely expensive CERN in Switzerland, the world's largest particle physics laboratory, could at a stretch be thought of as a social innovation) will develop in very different ways from ones with very low barriers to entry (like the millions of websites which have made use of the technologies invented at CERN).

But many of the patterns of social innovation are likely to be very different:

- There are likely to be very different motives, which may include material incentives but will almost certainly go far wider, to include motives of recognition, compassion, identity, autonomy and care.

- The critical resources are likely to be different: in businesses money provides the bottom line, but social innovations usually seek out a different mix of resources including political recognition and support, voluntary labour and philanthropic commitment.

- Social organisations tend to have different patterns of growth: as a rule they don't grow as fast as private ones, but they also tend to be more resilient.

- Judging success is also bound to be very different. Scale or market share may matter little for a social innovation concerned with a very intense but contained need. In some of the most radical social innovations participants' lives are dramatically improved by the act of collaboration, such as in is the reorganisation of social care as self-directed support.[47]

These are all reasons why there is a need for more rigour, sharper concepts, and clearer metrics.

Existing research on social innovation and related fields

Fortunately this is not a completely barren territory. There have been many case studies of social innovations within different fields (including health, education and criminal policy) and useful attempts have been made to understand social innovation in some universities, including Stanford (which publishes a 'Social Innovation Review'), Fuqua and Harvard (where the Kennedy School has run an extensive programme on innovations in governance). However, though suggestive, these have focused on individual case studies rather than investigating common patterns or aggregating learning.[48] As such they have not yet provided widely acknowledged models, or sufficient practical insights for practitioners: often rich accounts of individual social innovations do not add up to a clear picture of patterns (and generally the quality of theoretical work in this field has been low – with little progress since the pioneering work in the 1980s at Manchester and Sussex Universities linking social innovation to broader patterns of technological change). Nor has much use been made of the advances made in parallel disciplines.

As well as the study of innovation in economics and science there is an emerging, yet still small, body of research into the capacity of formally constituted social organisations (non-profits, NGOs, charities, voluntary and community organisations) to innovate in the delivery of public services[49] and, to build up innovative capacity more widely.[50] However such research (whilst extremely valuable) tests one sector's putative innovative capacity not the wider territory of social innovation. The only (and excellent) piece of original research we found into the UK voluntary sector's innovative capacity concluded that voluntary organisations are, 'better at believing they are innovative than being innovative'[51]. There is also some limited emerging work on the replication of successful voluntary sector initiatives[52] – which, though valuable, investigates one aspect of the process of innovation in isolation from its wider and precursory elements.

Considerable work is now under way on measuring the outputs and outcomes of public and social organisations, including the fascinating work led by Dale Jorgensen at MIT on valuing the informal economy and family work, and the recent work led by Tony Atkinson at Oxford University on the value of public services. These go far beyond the rather crude claims that are sometimes made for the productivity and efficacy of social organisations. (One leading figure in the social enterprise field, for example, has repeatedly suggested that the social sector is experiencing a rapid jump in productivity, and cites as evidence the fast growth of jobs numbers in civic organisations in countries like Germany and USA. The growth in jobs is fairly well-attested; but to link it to rising productivity is at best a non-sequitur, at worst economically illiterate. A more honest comment might be that we know very little about whether civic productivity is rising, falling or flat.) But they have yet to generate reliable metrics for the social or civic value that social organisations create.

The global umbrella organisations supporting social entrepreneurs and civic action – notably Civicus and Ashoka – have chosen to remain in an advocacy and promotional stance (giving primacy to civic organisations in the first case, and a largely individualistic model of change driven by social entrepreneurs in the latter). They have done a great deal to promote wider understanding of civic activism, and have provided invaluable support for many individuals and organisations across the world. But they have done less to advance serious knowledge about *how* social change takes place, or to engage with the new insights from economics and technology. Meanwhile within academia, centres at Harvard, Oxford and elsewhere are beginning to put the study of social enterprise (understood as the technique of trading in the market to achieve social aims) and social entrepreneurship (understood as the use of entrepreneurial skills to achieve a social purpose but not necessarily involving social enterprise) onto a surer footing[53]. However, whilst social innovation certainly occurs through social enterprise and social entrepreneurship it also happens in many other contexts. Conversely, although social entrepreneurship often involves innovation, only a small minority of social entrepreneurs create new models that can then be scaled up, and that process of scaling up often involves governments and larger businesses.

Another relevant body of work comes from the study of social investment (providing a range of debt through to equity products to social purpose organisations) stemming from progressive practice in philanthropy, for-profit banking and venture capital[54]. This work is valuable in illuminating the potential for different kinds of support – but it remains in its infancy in understanding how portfolios of different kinds of risk could be assembled and the perspective of financial investments naturally tend to favour models that can already demonstrate either public demand, or the prospect of public sector contracts. Genuinely radical innovations can rarely do either.

In short, whilst there is plenty of knowledge to draw on, the whole is less than the parts. In a preliminary survey of research undertaken across the world we have found no quantitative analysis systematically identifying inhibitors and critical success factors at each stage of the social innovation cycle. Nor have we found work specifically analysing the role that policy makers, funders and universities can play in supporting the process of social innovation.

Why what we don't know matters

A Google search on the word 'innovation' in March 2006 throws up some 780 million web pages, ranging from articles to toolkits, books to consultancies. By contrast a search for 'social innovation' generates only 415,000, i.e. approximately 0.05% of the total – a sign of how marginal this field remains.

We believe that the absence of sustained and systematic analysis is holding back the practice of social innovation. Specifically, a lack of knowledge makes it harder to see the main gaps in current provision of funding, advice and support. This is likely to result in fewer potential innovations being initiated. A lack of knowledge about common patterns is almost certain to make it harder for innovators themselves to be effective and for ideas to be improved into a sustainable form.

We know that some of the critical success factors for social innovation include strong leadership, clear mission, sensitivity to markets and users, and lean and flexible design. But much more work needs to be done to really understand and evidence the *precise* ways in which social innovation can best be supported.

More generally we need to better understand:

- The key gaps in particular sectors, and whether, for example, there is an excess of experimentation relative to take-up or vice versa.

- The best balance between very speculative funding of new ideas and investment in the growth of part-proven innovations.

- How best to straddle the innovation chasm – between promising ideas and large scale implementation.

- Appropriate and acceptable ratios of risk – are the patterns from venture capital or creative industries relevant, and if so what are the implications for investment?

- The best ways of refining and testing innovations - for example, in incubators or as offshoots of existing organisations.

- The relationships between organisational forms and creativity - for example, do boards of trustees tend to inhibit it?

- The best ways of using visionary founders – and moving them to one side if they lack management skills or become rigid in their thinking.

- The role of different electoral systems in encouraging political competition and social innovation.

- The precise merits and challenges of service users and existing providers being involved at differing stages of the innovation process.

The absence of knowledge also makes it harder for the various bodies that fund potential new solutions (ranging from government departments to independent foundations) to refine and explain their own strategies, in turn restricting the means of incubating promising ideas. Many funders now want to support innovation, and there are large public funds as well as foundation programmes targeted at this area and deliberately aimed at promising new ideas. But, without exception, the people running these funds admit in private that they lack much knowledge on which to base their decisions and practices, and have to rely instead on hunches or judgements about individuals.

What next: an agenda for action

Throughout this manifesto we have argued that social innovation is too little understood and too often left to chance. Business and science no longer depend on obdurate individuals and teams battling against the odds to get their ideas accepted. Instead they recognise that more systematic approaches pay dividends. A similarly systematic approach is long overdue in relation to social issues. If social innovation continues to be left to chance the risk is that pressing social problems will worsen; barriers (from congestion to climate change) will increasingly constrain economic growth; and the costs of key sectors (like health, the largest industry of the 21st century) will rise while their effectiveness stagnates.

Governments, foundations, businesses, NGOs and universities all have distinct roles to play in encouraging innovation. But a more systematic approach to generating and growing new ideas also requires new ways for them to work together, at least some of the time. Just as silicon provides a stable, and replicable, matrix which enables electronic components to work together efficiently, so do we need new models which enable social inventors, entrepreneurs and big organisations to work together more effectively. There is a particular need for intermediary organisations that can link 'bees' and 'trees' - the social entrepreneurs and inventors on the one hand and big governments, big business, big finance and big NGOs on the other.

Some countries have introduced welcome new support for individual social entrepreneurs, community projects and pilots. But these still fall well short of what is needed, and without systemic conditions for innovations to evolve and spread, most are bound to be crushed by existing vested interests, or at best to remain no more than interesting pilots.

In what follows we therefore turn to the new methods and structures which may be needed to put social innovation on a firmer footing.

Finance focused on innovation

In the very best organisations innovation becomes mainstream and people at every level are open to ideas and quick to seize new opportunities. Funding and investment automatically gravitate to the most promising innovations. But in the great majority of organisations this doesn't happen. Instead innovation depends on dedicated people and teams, with a license to explore new possibilities. We believe that the field of social innovation needs its own dedicated supports, even if in the long run innovation may be so integrated into the DNA of governments and NGOs that these are no longer needed.

These need money. Bright ideas may appear to emerge from thin air, but the business of innovation invariably involves costs to generate ideas, test them out and then to adapt them in the light of experience. In business, a significant proportion of funding for innovation comes from governments – through grants, tax credits for R&D and subsidies, alongside investment within companies and through dedicated investment vehicles, ranging from technology oriented venture capital to banks.

An equivalent mix of funding sources is needed for social innovation, for experiments, start ups and then for growth. Some of that will need to come from government, drawing on the experience of funds like the UK government's Invest to Save Budget and Futurebuilders. Some will need to come from foundations, which have greater freedom to experiment, and to target unfashionable and politically controversial fields. Some will need to come from more commercial funds drawing on the experience of venture capital funds such as Bridges Community Ventures in the UK and Pacific Community Ventures in the US (though these are bound to be less suitable for higher risk and more radical ventures which cannot demonstrate a prospective income stream), and from the growing field of venture philanthropy which is providing debt and quasi-equity finance alongside grants[55] (a list of the key forms of finance is provided in this endnote[56]). Looking to the future, these are some of the elements that would form a more mature social innovation system:

- Public (and foundation) funding for high risk 'blue skies' R&D in priority areas, deliberately aiming to generate a wide range of options that can be tested, observed, adapted and improved, with an assumption that a significant proportion will not work.

- Public agencies, foundations and individual philanthropists providing core funding for intermediary bodies like innovation laboratories, that can then provide a mix of development and financial support (we describe some of these in the next section).

- More public and private funding for organisational start-ups, recognising that there are likely to be quite high failure rates – and quick learning of lessons.

- Venture capital firms and angel investors becoming more sophisticated in their understanding of the dynamics of social enterprise, including higher risk and potentially high social reward ideas.

- More sophisticated metrics to assess investment prospects and results achieved in a way compatible with innovation, such as rapid learning and evolution of end goals during prototyping and start-up.

- Expert user laboratories to test out ideas, with the close involvement of users.

- Technology labs focused specifically on social uses, focused on key areas of technology that have been underused for social purposes, such as mobile telephony, artificial intelligence and Global Positioning Systems.

- More developed markets for social solutions, including outcome based funding models (which reward organisations for, for example, cutting recidivism, keeping people in jobs or improving the experience of chronic disease sufferers) and greater competition and contestability.

New dedicated social innovation accelerators

The second related priority is to encourage the spread of new centres to incubate and accelerate new ideas. Although there are many funds supporting individuals and small NGOs there are none with a focus on innovation, and none providing detailed, hands-on support to shape projects and improve their prospects of success. There are various incubators of social ventures already in existence such as Singapore's incubator for e-government ideas or Social Fusion, a California-based incubator for social enterprises. There are also a growing number of sources of support for individual social entrepreneurs, including funding and support organisations such as Ashoka and UnLtd – The Foundation for Social Entrepreneurs, and educators such as the School for Social Entrepreneurs and the Skoll Centre for Social Entrepreneurship at Said Business School. The Young Foundation's Launchpad programme is aiming to go beyond these by taking a more active role in the identification of needs and the design of new organisations as well as their incubation and launch, with a particular focus on ideas that have the potential to be scaled up (the methods used by Launchpad are described in more detail in the annex).

A related approach is to develop 'sectoral accelerators' for particular sectors, such as health and education, with an emphasis on scaleable innovations. These are most likely to work in sectors where public provision is dominant and where a government can see the advantage of speeding up innovation. They are also most likely to be useful where there is scope for innovation that crosses sectoral and disciplinary boundaries – as is the case with services for chronic illness, diet, fitness and mental health.

Such accelerators would: provide development funding for social entrepreneurs, groups of public sector workers, private companies and academics, as well as partnerships; rapidly test out new ideas in practice, with quick assessments; allow fast learning across a community of innovators; and establish clear pathways for scaling up the most promising models. They would be more like a development agency than a traditional reactive fund and would play a very active role in the advancement of knowledge and the emergence of new models (more details of how these might work are contained in the annex).

A parallel idea ('city accelerators') is being developed for cities with methods for identifying pressing needs. This involves scanning for promising solutions (from around the world as well as from people living within the city); testing them out in practice; and then applying them. These too are likely to work best where they can provide support for a wide range of types of organisation and project – from teams of public sector staff to NGOs and businesses – and where they have the clear support of political leaders in the city (again, more details are set out in the annex).

National and cross-national pools

At the national level, innovation also needs its own homes. No contemporary government has yet worked out how to promote social innovation. Hopefully none will try to monopolise it. We see the most promising practices as combining some of the elements described above (incubators, targeted funds tied to individual sectors as well as cross-cutting priorities) alongside funding tied to outcomes rather than outputs and activities, decentralisation to promote diversity and competition amongst a plurality of approaches where appropriate. These then need to be tied together by government-supported collaboratives ('innovation pools') to share learning and emerging insights (including better ways to recapture lessons from past innovations and experiments, many of which may have been ahead of their time).

Since so many challenges cut across national boundaries we also favour cross national innovation pools which bring together a group of interested governments or foundations from several countries for an aligned innovation process. The precursor for this exists in the closed groups of cities that share data and experiences on transport systems. An equivalent, for example for employment for the over-50s, would agree a common research programme, undertake parallel pilots, enable mutual learning between the people involved, (both those on the receiving end of the programme and those delivering it) and carry out joint assessment of the results.

Research and faster learning

To inform practical initiatives we also need much more extensive, rigorous, imaginative and historically aware research on how social innovation happens and how it can be helped. Alongside greater conceptual clarity and common definitions we need more case studies and better analysis of critical success factors and potential inhibitors at each stage of the innovation process, better links with adjacent disciplines working on private sector innovation and science, public sector improvement, and civil society, as well as research on some of the specifics of social innovation – for example on its links to faith; on which styles of philanthropy achieve the greatest long-term impact; how business CSR can best contribute to scaleable and replicable models; or how the use of new internet based business models can address social challenges.

A global network for action and research

This manifesto is deliberately preliminary; it describes a work in progress and is in part designed to bring together others interested in taking this work forward.

The ideas set out in this manifesto are already shaping much of the work that the Young Foundation is doing. We have already drawn in a wide range of global companies – including BP, Morgan Stanley, Cisco, Philips Design, Vertex and SAP; progressive foundations including Joseph Rowntree, Baring and Barrow Cadbury; and universities including LSE, UCL, Tsinghua and Melbourne.

This work also overlaps closely with work being done by a wide range of other organisations around the world. These include SITRA in Finland and Mandag Morgen, the Copenhagen Institute for Future Studies and Learning Lab in Denmark; Demos, the British Council, the International Futures Forum and the Design Council in the UK; the Centre for Comparative Political Economy in Beijing which runs a major annual prize for local innovations; the Institute for Smart Governance in Hyderabad and the Centre for Knowledge Societies in Bangalore; the Doors of Perception Network in the Netherlands; the Kennedy School at Harvard University; the pan-European EMUDE network coordinated from Milan; and the Baltic Design Network around the Baltic sea.[57]

There are also dozens if not thousands of organisations working on practical social innovation in health, education, the law, welfare and poverty and the environment with important insights to offer. Our interest lies in finding ways to enhance this disparate community, and to develop:

- Common ways of understanding social innovation.

- Common methods for supporting social innovation that are widely understood and easily digested, and that work well in creating real social value for institutions (governments, foundations, NGOs) and communities.

Our aim will be to develop ways for these insights to be shared – through a new global network that will be initiated with conferences in Beijing and London in 2006 and followed with Wikis, websites and publications, as well as practical projects and new enterprises.[58]

We believe that this work is long overdue and that social innovation badly needs to be taken from the fragmented margins into the centre of how we think about change and progress. Our prediction is within the next 20 to 40 years the innovative capacity of societies and governments will become at least as an important differentiator of national success than the innovative capacity of economies. As that happens, and 'Social Silicon Valleys' start to take shape, new tools will be needed, new skills and new kinds of organisation. These will be needed because social needs are not diminishing – and in many fields, from ageing to climate change - they are getting more acute.

All societies have remarkable capacities for myopia, obduracy and inertia. But this innovation gap should focus the minds of politicians, business, foundations and NGOs on the need to raise their game and hopefully the ideas set out here will help them to do so.

Annex: tools for accelerating social innovation

Launchpad

Launchpad combines in one place a design studio, incubator and innovation champion, and we believe this could be the model of other social innovation centres. As a design studio Launchpad:

- Takes projects from the very earliest stage of innovation – generation or discovery, refinement and filtering of concepts.

- Is strategic in about the problems we seek to address, based on evidence of unmet needs and identification of new opportunities to address these needs arising from new technologies, empirical understanding, political climate or consumer attitudes.

- Acts as a cross-pollinator across different sector and functional silos to catalyse the development of a new innovation – as a visualiser of possible new developments that may be outside current thinking and experience of any established institutions.

- Designs and develops new social ventures and their services taking an interdisciplinary and collaborative approach.

As an incubator Launchpad:

- Takes new ventures all the way through to launch and growing to scale.

- Develops a portfolio of projects, combining ones with greater potential impact and greater risk with ones with more immediate potential.

- Applies a robust development process including rigorous investigation of likely business models and rapid iterations of user testing with design modifications as part of quick, flexible piloting and prototyping.

- Brokers the necessary management and entrepreneurial talent, expert advice, finance, technology and corporate structures to launch independent ventures.

- Launches a series of new scaleable, sustainable ventures as nonprofits or for profits, sometimes with the aim of migrating back into the public sector and sometimes working on joint ventures with businesses or NGOs.

As an innovation champion Launchpad:

- Uses its portfolio of projects to promote social innovation in itself in order to galvanise support for individual projects.

- Attracts funding and in-kind support for early stage development of themed groups of projects.

- Works with key stakeholders to build their support to launch and scale up or replicate individual innovations.

- Hopes to inspire others by example to promote and practice social innovation, including taking up concepts that Launchpad itself does not have the capacity or capability to implement.

Our portfolio of projects covers fields including: asylum seekers, cross-cultural understanding, new communities of mutual support, affordable high quality childcare, new model schools, affordable access to justice, rehabilitation of ex-offenders and web-based innovations including user feedback mechanisms for public service providers. For more information see the Launchpad space on the Young Foundation website.

Sectoral innovation accelerators: health as an example

The idea of a Health Innovation Accelerator has been developed by the Young Foundation in dialogue with the Department of Health, the Design Council RED team, and a group of local agencies and practitioners.[59] It aims to achieve rapid design, testing and implementation of ideas in relation to chronic disease – much faster than would be possible with formal pilots, and with much more creativity than would be possible within bureaucracies.

The background to the HIA is: recognition of the rising incidence of chronic disease – arthritis, diabetes and mental illness; the fact that once acute conditions like cancer and heart disease are becoming more like chronic conditions; huge resulting cost pressures on health systems at every level; clear evidence of patient dissatisfaction; inadequate existing models; and the emergence of radically different models for supporting sufferers, with much more power and control in the hands of patients supported by an infrastructure of medical care, information, but also mutual support from other patients. (For more detail see Geoff Mulgan's lecture on health on the Young Foundation website which sets out eight likely characteristics of new models of health care.[60])

Areas covered include new models to put commissioning power into the hands of groups suffering from chronic disease; new models for helping the mentally ill into jobs; new methods of handling radically different health belief systems in diverse cities; new roles for coaches to help people manage their own health; and new web based models linking 'expert patients' with others suffering similar health and life challenges.

A related issue is the 50% of the cost of health care that comes in the last six months of life. This high cost coincides with evidence that many terminally ill patients are uncomfortable about the imbalance between the effort devoted to extending life (partly because of fears of litigation and because of the Hippocratic Oath) and the reluctance to allow them to control the manner of their own death.

These background conditions give good grounds for believing that some very different models are likely to grow up over the next few years, offering better health outcomes, better patient experience and lower cost. But existing health organisations are ill-suited to the job of innovation, despite some good work done by programmes like the NHS Expert Patients Programme. The HIA aims to provide a more systematic approach to innovating and testing new models in practice, using a range of methods including:

- Working in partnership with the key decision-makers within the NHS at a national level whose support any new innovations will need and with the key local NHS organisations and businesses needed to prototype and pilot new innovations.

- Focusing on priority needs as identified through independent research, user surveys and policy debates within government and the NHS.

- Mobilising users and patients themselves to identify existing informal solutions or promising avenues and then to provide input to rapid design iterations on user requirements and preferences.

- Scanning for neighbouring innovations or parallel fields from which lessons can be drawn, including new technologies.

- Using creativity methods of various kinds to turn these into products or rough ideas (for example using aspects of the IDEO methods for product design).

- Structured workshops with combinations of experts and non-expert entrepreneurs, technologists, community activists to identify potential solutions.

- Using the web to support a community of commentators and contributors in open source methods.

- Moving quickly into testing rough versions of these ideas in real life settings, rapidly adapting them until they can be taken a stage further and then using metrics to test against outcome goals, subjective experience.

- Turning successful ideas either into practices that can be mainstreamed in existing primary care provision or into new businesses or social enterprises.

In some sectors these accelerators will need to operate to coordinate many players. For example to shift cities and nations over to radically changed transport technologies will require coordination of businesses, public purchasing, civil society and campaigns and finance for members of the public alongside fast-track innovation of new models.

Innovation acceleration in cities

Many cities and nations have been through periods of intense creativity in the past, mobilising the minds and imaginations of their citizens. We have been developing more systematic methods which draw on these past experiences but help cities and small nations to raise their game. These methods include:

- Analytical tools for mapping needs. The Young Foundation has developed a novel methodology which draws on the many attempts over the last two centuries (including classic 19th century studies by Booth and Rowntree) and innovative methods used in developing countries. These aim to combine the capture of statistical data, observations of front line agencies and the insights of people and communities themselves, recognising them as competent interpreters of their own lives.

- Lateral analysis - designing ways of looking at a city that invite new trains of thinking. For example, analysis showed that Berlin was nine times more bio diverse than the surrounding countryside, which opened up new ways of thinking about how the city's green spaces could be organised.

- Methods for involving large groups in considering priorities and options including: deliberative polls, participatory budgeting and Planning for Real. (This is a field with a burgeoning array of methods, including a range of social softwares with reputational devices).

- Seeking 'positive deviants' within the city itself and finding ways to generalise their experiences.

- Identifying promising ideas from elsewhere – since a majority of relevant ideas are bound to be in existence already along with creative methods for generating new ideas.

- Re-linking the city inhabitants in new ways including: home tourism; twinning of schools with workplaces; shared tasks; mobilising schoolchildren for public tasks (for example, inventories of equipment which could be used in emergencies).

- Methods for testing in real or controlled environments including: innovation funds, incubators, zones, pilots, pathfinders, along with methods for assessing success, and then for adapting and scaling up.

By combining these methods, we are able to generate creative energy, focus it on the key needs and maximise the prospects of the resulting ideas actually being implemented on the ground. Sometimes these throw up entirely new solutions. Sometimes they make it possible to bring two problems together to make a solution – for example, employing isolated old people to provide watching eyes over streets and parks; or employing workless young people to provide safe late night transport. Generally these require dedicated teams working alongside existing agencies, but with authority from the top (the chief executive, Mayor or political leader), to break through barriers.

References

[1] Helpman, E. (2004) *The Mystery of Economic Growth*, Cambridge, MA. Following on from Solow's work Elhanan Helpman estimated that differences in knowledge and technology explain more than 60% of the differences among countries in income and growth rates.

[2] Rare exceptions include Pinter, F. (1985) *Stimulating Innovation: A Systems Approach* Tudor Rickards; Gerhuny, J (1983) *Social Innovation and the Division of Labour* OUP; Njihoff, M. (1984) *The Political Economy of Innovation* The Hague, Kingston

[3] For example his book: Young, M. (1983) '*The Social Scientist as Innovator*', Cambridge, Mass.

[4] www.spartacus.schoolnet.co.uk; www.bbc.co.uk/history. Chadwick's wider role in British society was, unfortunately, far less progressive.

[5] There have been many attempts to define an overarching theory of social (or economic) change. These theories were particularly fashionable in the 19th century – change was explained through elaborate theories focused on the impact of technology, contradictions, class struggle, or the advance of reason, and there were also more simplistic theories which ascribed change to visionary individuals or national will. More recently there have been various attempts to define an overarching 'theory of change' (and in economics to offer a synthetic theory of growth). However, all theories of this kind are based on a simple error: although every aspect of social life is connected, there are no good reasons for believing that a single theory could explain phenomena as diverse as family life, urban communities, the evolution of workplaces, identity and conflict, crime and violence, exploitation and cooperation. They are different in nature, have their own logics, rhythms, and any general theory is likely to be either banal or wrong. Even within economics overarching theories of change and growth have not fared well compared to more modest theories focused on such things as the dynamics of labour markets or monetary policy. The big social changes that have accompanied industrialisation have had some common features: urbanisation; changed gender roles; the rise of mass media; globalisation; political empowerment of previously marginalised groups and so on. It is also possible to point to some common themes in the stories of social change: the role of blockages and impediments in galvanising change; the role of ideas in giving shape to these and turning personal resentments into social forces; the role of new knowledge in making things possible – from technologies like the car or genomics, to the knowledge about health that has motivated anti-smoking campaigns. There are also parallel struggles for resources – political, economic, cultural – and parallel stories about how new ideas and movements try to attract others. But these cannot be summarised into a simple model (for example, by analogy with evolutionary theories) that have any explanatory or predictive power, despite many attempts. We believe that it is possible to provide more accurate analyses and descriptions of how new models, programmes and organisations emerge and spread, how they crystallise, are concentrated in a model and are then amplified, and our expectation is that new insights will come from gathering examples, studying the fine-grained detail as much as from abstract theory. Anyone wanting to achieve social change also needs to have thought through how they think change happens – and how they can influence major interests and public excitement, how they can circumvent barriers, and what might be realistic timescales for change. But we are neither advocating, nor expecting, an overarching theory.

[6] www.robert-owen.com; www.newlanark.org

[7] The Octavia Hill Birthplace Museum – www. octaviahillmuseum.org

[8] For a good overview of his work see Dench, G., Flower, T. and Gavron, K. (2005) *Young at Eighty : the prolific public life of Michael Young,* Carcanet Press, Manchester. For a full biography see Briggs, A. (2001) *Michael Young: Social Entrepreneur,* Palgrave Macmillan, London

[9] Bornstein, D. (2004) *How to change the world: social entrepreneurs and the power of new ideas,* Oxford University Press, Oxford

[10] Childline was founded in Bombay in 1996; by 2002 the organisation was working in thirty cities. A full account is available in Bornstein, D. (2004) op cit.

[11] Renascer provides care to poor children after they are discharged from hospital. By 2002, Renascer had assisted 6,000 children and successor organisations a further 10,000 people. Now the challenge is to transform Renascer into a reference and training centre spawning and supporting cells across Brazil. A full account is available in Bornstein, D. (2004) op cit.

[12] CIDA believes itself to be the only 'free', open-access, holistic, higher educational facility in the world which is operated and managed by its students, from administration duties to facilities management. Two additional key features are partnerships with a great number of businesses in the design and delivery of all programmes - and the requirement of every student to return to their rural schools and communities, during holidays, to teach what they have learnt. A full account is available in Bornstein, D. (2004) op cit. See also www.cida.co.za; Lucille Davie writing on www.joburg.org.za; and Andrea Vinassa writing on www.workinfo.com.

[13] http://en.wikipedia.org/wiki/History_of_feminism

[14] www.disabilityhistory.org; http://bancroft.berkeley.edu/collections/drilm/;
http://americanhistory.si.edu/disabilityrights/

[15] For the comparisons between business and the social sector in making organisations great see www.jimcollins.com/

[16] For example, http://james.parkinsons.org.uk/uk.htm

[17] A recent article in the Economist can be found at
/www.economist.com/business/displaystory.cfm?story_id=5624944

[18] For example, de Bono, E. (1970) *Lateral Thinking - Creativity Step by Step,* Perennial Library London, and many others.

[19] See www.globalideasbank.org/site/home/. The top 500 ideas that will change the world are at www.globalideasbank.org/site/store/detail.php?articleId=178. A list of similar organisations can be found at www.stuartcdoddinstitute.org/innovationlinks.shtml

[20] Useful websites include:
Poverty Action Lab www.povertyactionlab.org/;
Social Action Laboratory www.psych.unimelb.edu.au/research/labs/soc_actionlab.html;
Affirmative Action Laboratory www.naledi.org.za/pubs/2000/indicator/article4.htm;
Innovation Lab Copenhagen www.innovationlab.net/sw4918.asp;
Civic Innovation Lab www.civicinnovationlab.org/;
Eastman Innovation Lab www.eastman.com/innovationlab/
MIT Community Innovation Lab http://web.mit.edu/cilab/;
ETSU Innovation Lab www.etsu.edu/innovationlab/

[21] Mulgan, G 'Government and Knowledge', in Evidence and Policy Journal, 2005

[22] The project did survive for several years in Milton Keynes in England. But it never took off.

[23] Markides, C. and Geroski, P. (2005) *Fast Second: how smart companies bypass radical innovation to enter and dominate new markets,* Jossey-Bass, San Francisco

[24] www.barnardos.org.au/barnardos/html/innovations.cfm

[25] Wingham, R. (1997) *Guaranteed electronic markets: The backbone of the twenty first century economy?,* Demos, London. This book described a sophisticated new form of market that could be organised on the web, and which is now being piloted in east London.

[26] Christianson, C. (2003) *The Innovators Solution,* Harvard Business School Press, Cambridge Mass.

[27] For example, a review of the literature on organisational innovation identified 6,240 articles published between 1980 and 1994 alone. Wolfe, RA. (1994) Organisational innovation: review, critique and suggested research directions *Journal of Management Studies* 31 (3) pp. 405-431. For a more recent literature review see Reed, R. (1999) Determinants of Successful Organisational Innovation: A Review of Current Research *Journal of Management Practice* Jan-June 2000.

[28] Walker RM, Jeanes, E. and Rowlands, RO. (2002) 'Measuring Innovation – applying the literature-based innovation output indicator to public services' *Public Administration* 80 10 pp.201-214

[29] Albury, D. and Mulgan, G. (2003) *Innovation in the Public Sector,* Strategy Unit, London

[30] As identified by Damapnour, F. (1987) The Adoption of Technological, Administrative and Ancillary innovations: Impact of Organisational Factors in *Journal of Management,* 13, 4 pp.675 -688

[31] The best recent survey of the field is Nooteboom, B. (2001) *Learning and Innovation in organisations and economies,* Oxford University Press, which provides a very sophisticated overview both of the sociology and economics of innovation

[32] Two good general sources are the Stanford Project on Emerging Companies www.gsb.stanford.edu/SPEC/index.html and Innovation and Entrepreneurship http://knowledge.wharton.upenn.edu/index.cfm?fa=viewCat&CID=12

[33] Albury, D. and Mulgan, G. (2003) *Innovation in the Public Sector,* Strategy Unit, London p.26

[34] Murmann, JP (2004) *Knowledge and Competitive Advantage*, EH.NET; von Hippel, E (2005) *Democratising Innovation* MIT Press Cambridge Mass; Baumol, R (2003) *The Free-Market Innovation Machine: Analyzing the Growth of Miracle Capitalism*, Princeton University Press

[35] Lester, R and Piore, M (2004) *Innovation – The Missing Dimension* Harvard University Press Cambridge Mass

[36] See Rogers, EM (1995) *Diffusion of Innovations* Free Press New York; Nutley, S Davies, H and Walter, I (2002) *Learning from the Diffusion of Innovations* University of St Andrews; Nooteboom B (2000) *Learning and innovation in organisations and economies* Oxford University Press, Oxford

[37] Smith-Doerr L et al (1999) 'Networks and Knowledge Production: Collaboration and Patenting in Bio-Technology' in Leenders AJ and Gabbay SM (eds) *Corporate Social Capital and Liability cited in* Noteboom B (2001) op cit

[38] For example, Moss Kanter, R. (2001) *Evolve! Succeeding in the digital culture of tomorrow* Harvard Business School Press, Cambridge, Mass.

[39] For example, Kao J (1991) *The Entrepreneurial Organisation,* Prentice Hall, New Jersey, and *Jamming*

[40] For example, Braben, D. (2004) *Pioneering Research: A Risk Worth Taking,* Wiley

[41] For example, Hamel, G. (2000) *Leading The Revolution,* Penguin, New York

[42] For example, Follett, MP (1924) *Creative Experience*, New York

[43] John Hagel and John Seely Brown, 'Connecting globalisation and innovation: some contrarian perspectives', paper prepared for World Economic Forum 2006

[44] Von Hippel, E (2005) *Democratising Innovation,* MIT. Leadbeater, C (2006) The user innovation revolution, National Consumer Council

[45] Mulgan, G. and Steinberg, T. (2005) *Wide Open: the potential of open source methods*, Demos and the Young Foundation, London

[46] See http://en.wikipedia.org/wiki/Reverse_engineering for an interesting discussion of property rights and innovation

[47] In the UK, the In Control pilots delivered under the government's policy Valuing People and now recommended for wider adoption are a good examples of innovation in the a new relationship between user and suppliers *Improving the Life Chances of Disabled People,* Prime Minister's Strategy Unit, January 2005 p.93; 'Controlling interest', David Brindle in Society Guardian, March 2nd 2005; www.selfdirectedsupport.org

[48] Stanford Social Innovation Review - www.ssireview.com; The Social Innovation Forum - www.wfs.org/innovate.htm; Government Innovators Network - www.innovations.harvard.edu; www.changemakers.net; Drucker NonProfit Innovation Discovery Site - www.pfdf.org/innovation/

[49] For example: Alcock, P., Barnwell, T. and Ross, L. (2004) *Formality or Flexibility? Voluntary Sector Contracting,* NCVO, London; Osborne, S (1998) *Voluntary Organisations and Innovation in Public services,* Routledge, London

[50] Evans, E. and Saxton, J. (2004) *Innovation rules! A roadmap to creativity and innovation for not-for-profit organisations*, NFP Synergy, London

[51] ibid

[52] Leat, D (2003) *Replicating Successful Voluntary Sector Projects,* Association of Charitable Foundations London; Community Action Network's beanstalk programme – www.can-online.org.uk

[53] For example: Amin, A., Cameron, A. and Hudson, R. (2002) *Placing the Social Economy,* Routledge, London; Westall, A. (2001) *Value Led, Market Driven* IPPR London; Pharaoh, C (2004) *Social enterprise in the balance,* Charities Aid Foundation, West Malling

[54] For example: at www.davidcarrington.net/articles.php; Peacock, Geraldine et al, (2003) *The Magic Roundabout – how charities can make their money go further: an introduction to programme related investment*, Bircham Dyson Bell, London; Bolton, M. (2004) *New approaches to funding not for profit organisations: a snapshot*, Charities Aid Foundation, West Malling.

[55] As above

[56] The seven main sources of social investment are:
- Specialist investors established specifically to provide capital to under-capitalised geographical communities, such as Bridges Community Ventures
- Specialist lenders established specifically to provide capital to civil society organisations, such as Futurebuilders
- Specialist divisions of mainstream banking institutions
- Venture capital funds targeting businesses pursuing social goals alongside profits (such as Climate Change Capital)
- Government investment agencies
- Individual philanthropists or angel investors
- Grant making foundations (through mission related investments)

[57] www.balticdesigntransfer.com

[58] For example, the world bank's 'social innovation' blog
http://psdblog.worldbank.org/psdblog/2006/02/social_and_envi.html

[59] This work has drawn on a long tradition of radical innovation in health (in which Michael Young played an important role), some of which led to the creation of the Expert Patients Programmes and the Health Collaboratives. *Co-creating health* (2004) by Charles Leadbeater and Hilary Cottam and published by the Design Council is an excellent account of the role that design can play in innovation.

[60] See www.youngfoundation.org.uk/?p=214

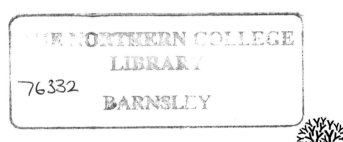